LADY OF THE MOUNTAIN HALL

A Skadi Devotional

Skadi, by "H.L.M." Foster and Cummings, *Asgard Stories* (1901)

LADY OF THE MOUNTAIN HALL

A Skadi Devotional

by Rev. Laura "Snow" Fuller

The Troth
2019

© 2019, The Troth. All rights reserved. No part of this book may be reproduced or transmitted in any form or by any means, electronic or mechanical, including photocopy, recording, or any information storage and retrieval system, without prior permission in writing from the publisher. Exceptions may be allowed for non-commercial "fair use," for the purposes of news reporting, criticism, comment, scholarship, research, or teaching.

Published by The Troth
325 Chestnut Street, Suite 800
Philadelphia, PA 19106
http://www.thetroth.org/

ISBN-13: 978-1-941136-31-7 (hardcover)
978-1-941136-30-0 (paperback)
978-1-941136-32-4 (e-book)

Cover layout: Ben Waggoner
Front cover photo: Matthew Kennedy
Mask carved by Timothy "Bjorn" Jones (https://www.BjornsWoodcarving.com)
Troth logo designed by Kveldúlfr Gundarsson, drawn by 13 Labs, Chicago, Illinois

Contents

Foreword	vi
Introduction	viii
Chapter 1: Introduction to Heathenry	2
What Does Heathen Mean?	2
Heathen Gods	4
Chapter 2: Skadi in the Lore	8
The *Prose Edda*	8
The *Poetic Edda*	12
Ynglinga Saga	18
Chapter 3: Social Norms	20
Skadi the Ring-Lady	20
Chapter 4: UPG	24
Health	25
Goddess of the Hunt	26
Personality: Cold, Logical and Warrior Trained	28
Her Family	28
Relationship with Ullr	29
Skadi and Gender Fluidity	30
The Bright Bride of Gods	30
The Venomous Snake	31
Her Magical Nature	32
Fylgia Magic	32
Mother of the Berserkers	34
Chapter 5: Poetry, Prayers, Journeys, and Rituals	37
Poetry and Prayers	37
Journeys	45
Rites	50
Conclusions	63
Works Cited	65
Sources of Illustrations	66

Foreword

The majority of this book has been written by Laura "Snow" Fuller, a cisgendered woman, regarding a goddess. That is to say, this book was written by a female regarding a female divinity. Further, it must be said the presumed audience for this book is largely other women. The author has written about history and lore, on one hand, and UPG and a modern cult, on the other hand – the latter not without a certain element of female empowerment. For Skadi is nothing if not empowering for those who heed her demanding cult.

There is a decided need for female friendly space and female empowerment in Heathenry/Ásatrú. All too often Heathen spaces cater to men with macho notions of Viking warrior prowess, a type pejoratively referred to as "Brosatrú." Many of my female acquaintances in Heathenry confess to feeling overwhelmed by such types. They perceive there is no space for them other than to play the part (and look the part) of the nubile young Viking woman in need of a strong man to defend her and seduce her. They have been reduced to second class citizens of the religion, good for nothing other than parading their sexuality, or perhaps serving beer and mead to the menfolk.

We have strong goddesses in our religion who call different types, all with valuable roles to play. Frigg is lady of the keep, granting clear counsel and presiding over the well-being of one's homestead and inner-yard. Freyja, a powerful personality if there ever was one, harkens to those who explore ecstasy, whether through magic or sexuality. And gentle Eir is ever ready to lend a healing hand to those who supplicate her.

Skadi, though, is very much a warrior, or at least a huntress. She demands the strength, both mental and physical, needed to survive in wild spaces. Like Artemis of the Greeks, her call is to women who will not necessarily be bound by the typical conventions of female domestic duties. The mountain, the woods, and the snow-capped fields are her domain.

Skadi's women will not be those who skulk demurely at the back of a Brosatrú Hall, having no agency beyond service to their male compatriots. Skadi's devotees are fierce and free, who gallivant gleefully through harsh climes that would kill others. And if a Skadi's woman decides to serve someone or something, it is because it is *her choice*, one that accords with her own values and has been contemplated through her own logical reflection. When a Skadi's woman commits to a person or to a cause, she invests it with all the fiber of her being, marshalling her will and strength to see it through. Woe betide anyone—man, woman or god!—that gets in her way.

But that is not to say Skadi accepts only women, nor is it to say only women may derive worth from the words presented here. There is indeed something for those who identify as male, a type of empowerment every bit as uplifting as that promised to women. One that is ennobled beyond the empty posturing and rank mindlessness of the macho Viking wannabes who sometimes throng Ásatrú.

If I could reduce Skadi's cultic demands to some pithy saying, it would be this: one must cultivate strength in body, mind and spirit. One must stand up for what is right, regardless of the consequences, and one must have the mental fortitude and physicality to endure the resulting struggles. It is not "might makes right," but might *for* right. The giantess who marched on all of Asgard to demand justice for her father demands nothing else.

Herein potentially lies a nobler concept of "manliness" than what is typically bandied about on the street. Manly virtue would consist not in bedding as many females as possible, nor would it be defined by testosterone-laden acts divorced from morality or strategy. Rather, a man's worth would be assessed to the degree he protected his family, his community, his just causes.

Skadi is not an emotional goddess. Her logic is as cold as the icy slopes of Thrymheim. She does not seduce or beguile. She does not pull at heart strings, nor make impassioned speeches replete with histrionics. She lays out what is needed in a clear, calm matter and details the steps needed to achieve one's goals. In that sense she plays a role similar to Athena of the Greeks — dispassionate counsel given to would-be heroes.

Skadi is no stranger to courage or strength. But that courage and strength is tethered to icy strategy, and harnessed in the service of justice and obligation. Therein lies an ideal that can elevate any gender.

— *Rev. Jeremy Baer, Redesperson and Clergy, The Troth*

Introduction

In 2011 when I took my first steps on this path, I felt like I was wandering about a bit lost. It started with four miscarriages, the last one on Easter Sunday. When I called my priest to come give comfort, the calls were never returned. This was followed shortly by the breaking of the child sex abuse scandals and a disgusting display by my fellow parishioners who began a campaign to support our priests. This prompted me to leave the Catholic Church in 2004.

Maybe you already know this, but religion becomes a part of a person's identity, and while leaving the church was very much the right thing for me to do, it left me with a bit of a hole in my soul. I joked about being a Recovering Catholic, but in truth I felt lost and alone.

By 2011, my marriage was falling apart, I had dropped out of graduate school, and was having trouble finding a job. I'd had a serious injury that had made movement a challenge, which had caused me to gain weight, which made movement even more of a challenge. . . life was in a downward spiral of helplessness and the only thing at the bottom was a bleak pit of depression.

And then it happened.

I was doing some research on Viking weddings with a friend. I don't even remember what prompted it now, but we came across a webpage that talked about the rebirth of Heathen practices and how people were reconstructing this ancient religion from texts and artifacts. My friend and I looked at each other with wide eyes and said at the same time, "THIS!"

Like many people who call themselves Heathen or Ásatrú, or any of the other names that have been given to this reconstructed religion, we found this path as adults. That meant we had a lot of catching up to do, and both of us went straight to the bookstore and bought every book on Norse mythology we could find. We spent the rest of the weekend reading them and by the time she left to go back home, we had decided to start a local group together and do what we could to connect with others.

In our research we found our way to The Troth, an international organization that is well known for its scholarship and its willingness to embrace any who would seek the Northern Gods. We also found out that not everyone walking our new path was so accepting. That was disturbing, but we were undaunted.

The other thing we soon found out was that while there are a number of surviving stories about the Northern gods (especially Thor and Odin and Loki), and while these gods were once spread over most of Northern Europe, there were few stories that survived about many of the goddesses among them, certainly not in any real depth. This was disappointing to us, as we both felt drawn to the idea of worshipping a goddess, someone we could relate to. In my case, it was something that grew out of my childhood love of Greek mythology in general and any story about Artemis in particular. I wanted a Norse version of Artemis, or at least one with similar characteristics. While Skadi is very, very different from Artemis in many ways, in the section of this book dealing with UPG, or Unverified Personal Gnosis, I will give some examples of how she has come over the years to fill the role for me of wild and demanding taskmistress who nonetheless supports her followers in a time of crisis.

The first chapter of this book is a brief overview of Heathenry, primarily for those who currently walk other paths. It shares a bit about the various types of Heathen practice in the modern age, the Gods, and the major surviving sources of information about them. It is not an exhaustive treatment of this, as there are plenty of good "intro" books out there.

The second chapter is a detailed look at the Norse legends in which Skadi makes an appearance. It is important that we ground our work in the surviving lore, as it gives us a baseline for the motivations of the Gods as understood by those who worshipped them a thousand and more years ago. One thing that I wish to emphasize is that it is my personal belief that modern understanding should make sense based on this ancient knowledge. Yes, people change. So do gods. But at the end of the day, or the era in this case, their underlying personality traits and motivations do not.

The third chapter examines some of the social structures of the time when the gods of the North ruled. This helps us to understand their stories, for they (both story and god) are a product of those times. Understanding the social climate is integral to understanding the story.

The fourth chapter is my own UPG (unverified personal gnosis) and that of others who have worked closely with Skadi. It is based on my experiences with Skadi in ritual and magic. As always, when someone is sharing this sort of experience, take it with a grain of salt. It works for me. It may not work for you. Or some parts may and other parts may not. That is okay. It is to be expected, even.

The fifth and final chapter is a set of rituals, prayers, and trance inductions to honor Her. They are meant to give the reader a place to begin, as often, having a pre-written script makes a practice seem approachable.

My hope for you in reading this book is that you feel comfortable approaching her. In my experience, she is a powerful ally and unwaveringly loyal friend. While her path is not easy and she demands much, she has much to give in return. Whether you currently consider yourself Heathen (or any of the other words we use for the reconstructed set of Northern religious practices), Wiccan, Pagan, or none of the above, I hope that you find what you seek.

—*Snow*

"Central Nordic" unequal skis from Norway. The shorter ski, or *andor*, was used for pushing forward, while the the longer ski, or *langski*, was used for gliding. This style of skis was in use at least from medieval times and probably back into prehistory, and it survived into the 20th century. Skadi's Norse name *öndur-dís* refers to the *öndur* or *andor*, the shorter ski for pushing onward. Anno Trysil Engerdal Museum TB.02627. Photo by Emir Curt, Creative Commons CC BY-SA 4.0.

Ring Lady
Fearless one
From mountain peak
Your will is done

When ice and snow
Cover the land
I call to you
To take my hand

Chapter 1: Introduction to Heathenry

What Does Heathen Mean?

There are a lot of good books that provide a thorough introduction to the modern practice of Heathenry. If you wish a more in-depth look at this subject, I can happily recommend *A Practical Heathen's Guide to Ásatrú* by Patricia Lafayllve. For our purposes, let us spend just a moment talking about what we mean by the term.

When we refer to Heathen practices, what we are talking about are the pre-Christian practices of the Germanic tribes. These tribes inhabited much of Northern and Western Europe including Scandinavia, continental Germany, the land of the Franks, Anglo-Saxon England, the Goths who invaded Rome and the Iberian Peninsula, all the way to Kiev in Russia. Any place a language from the Germanic language family tree was spoken, the influence of these traditions was felt. When we refer to Heathen practices, we are referring to an attempt to reconstruct the religions of this part of the world before they were decimated by Christianity's influence.

There are many words that are used today by those who engage in these practices. Heathen is something of a catch-all, but as people feel pulled to the practices of a specific culture within this Germanic umbrella, some choose other terms to describe what they do. While this is not intended to be an exhaustive list, I wish to delineate some of the more common.

The word Heathen is of Germanic origin. It was used to refer to those "of the heath." The uncouth, uneducated rural masses, whose pagan practices were the hardest for the Catholic Church to stamp out. Bonfires continued to burn in the countryside long after the aristocracy had converted for political and financial gains to the new religion, Christianity. In our modern context, most English speakers use it almost interchangeably with Pagan, but where Pagan has Latin origins, Heathen is Germanic. As this is a return to pre-Christian Germanic traditions, the term Heathen makes sense as a sort of umbrella term for this family of practices.

Some of the best-preserved stories of the northern gods come from Iceland, preserved in the *Eddas*. Iceland was one of the last countries to convert to Christianity, and the only one to do so peacefully, around the year 1000 CE. Because of this, it is also where the largest amount of lore was saved. There are two *Eddas*, the *Poetic Edda* and the *Prose Edda*. The *Poetic Edda* is a collection of stories, whereas the *Prose Edda* was written by Snorri Sturluson in the 1200s CE. Snorri was an educated Christian who was working to keep the poetic forms of his ancestors alive. As such, he is an important, if controversial, figure for many heathens. He did much to keep the old stories alive, but it is difficult to tell how much he changed them to align with his Christian worldview.

A popular name for one of the branches of Heathenry, based mostly on these Icelandic works, is Ásatrú. Ásatrú is a modern compound word taken from Icelandic and means "True to the Æsir." The Æsir is one of the tribes of gods in the Norse pantheon (the other being the Vanir). We know definitively which tribe some of the Northern Gods belonged to from the lore, but for many of them we can only guess. Based on the stories of the Eddas, the best known among the Æsir are Odin and Thor. In a similar vein, those who consider themselves under the patronage of one of the Vanir sometimes refer to themselves as Vanatrú. The most popular Vanir (based again on who is defined as such in the Eddas) are Freyja and Frey. Skadi only shows up in the Icelandic lore, but she is born to neither tribe. Instead, she is born to the tribe of Giants (*Jötnar*). Many of the other gods live among the Æsir, but we are never told which tribe they were born to.

Another set of labels people choose derive from the set of practices that were found in England during the Anglo-Saxon period. Many people simply call themselves Anglo-Saxon Heathens (and abbreviate this to ASH), while others prefer to use the Old English *fyrn sidu*, or Elder Customs. Note that *fyrn sidu* is a modern term, not one found in any Old English sources. Like Norse lore, much of what we know about AS pagan practice comes from a churchman, in this case, the Venerable Bede and his work *Ecclesiastical History of the English People*. For those interested in ASH, I would happily recommend the work of Alaric Albertsson as a starting point.

A third set of traditions comes from the Deitsch (Pennsylvania Dutch) communities in the United States and uses the term Urglaawe, meaning Primal Faith. Urglaawe combines the Teutonic pantheon in the context of the Deitsch (Pennsylvania German) culture with many beliefs from the traditional Deitsch culture, including pre-Christian facets of the healing practice of Braucherei and the folklore as handed down through the ages by word of mouth (Lusch-Schreiwer, "About Urglaawe").

One final set of practices I wish to touch on are Continental Heathen practices. Though Germany was converted early to Christianity and felt pressure even earlier due to their geographic closeness to the officially Christian Roman Empire, many of the folktales told today have pre-Christian origins and give us hints to the past. The brothers Grimm collected many of these tales and published them in the early 1800s CE. As Heathen practices make a return in Europe, these tales are a goldmine of information on the legends of the past. Another source dating to Roman times for information on the Continental tribes is found in Tacitus and his work *Germania*. Tacitus, who lived approximately 56-120 CE, was a Senator and Historian of the Roman Empire. His book *Germania* is an ethnographic work about the Germanic tribes outside the Roman Empire, with which the empire interacted. Tacitus himself did not venture into the German territories, though, and so his accounts are second hand. Also, while important, they must be read with an understanding that the Romans liked to build equivalencies between other cultures and their own, Romanizing names and practices. And so as many questions arise out of the work of Tacitus as are answered.

These are but a few of the titles and ways people formulate a Heathen practice. As this book is about Skadi and she only shows up in the Norse lore, I share this just to give a sense of the breadth and scope of the modern Heathen movement.

Heathen Gods

Though the various Germanic tribes had some differences in their pantheons, for the purpose of this work, I am going to focus on the Norse. That said, I will be using the common English spelling of the names of the gods and goddesses.

The leader of the Norse pantheon is Odin. He is frequently called the All-father, and of all the gods he has more bynames than any other. He is known to be a wanderer, the one who discovered the magic of the Runes, and the god who gives the gift of poetry to mankind. He rides the eight-legged horse Sleipnir. He chooses warriors who fall in battle to join him in Valhalla to prepare for Ragnarok, the battle in which many of the gods die. Odin is a master strategist, and he does nothing without a series of reasons. Evidence points to Odin being prominently worshipped by skalds (poets) and the nobility, and rarely by the common folk. It isn't surprising, then, that he is one of the gods for whom we have the most complete collection of stories. After all, skalds crafted the stories and princes paid them.

Odin is born of a line of Frost Giants, and he and his brothers create the world out of the body of Ymir, a primordial being. Odin is a sworn blood brother to Loki. We are told he swore an oath not to carouse unless Loki was also welcome, which is part of what sets up the story told in *Lokasenna*.

Loki is born a giant, and is unusual in that he takes a name derived from his mother's name, Laufey, rather than his father's name Farbauti. While patronymics were common among the Norse, matronymics were not. The name Laufeyson could refer to the fact that his father was unknown, or that his mother was the more important personage of the two. Either way, though, it sets Loki apart as having an unusual family from the start. Loki figures into a number of stories found in the *Eddas*, usually as a troublemaker who causes problems for the gods and then is forced to fix the problems, bringing new benefits along with the problems.

Odin's wife is Frigga. She is a daughter of earth and has her own hall, Fensalir. She sometimes sits on Odin's high seat, and so she knows everything that happens in the Nine Worlds, although she keeps it secret. Frigga has twelve handmaidens, about whom we know very little other than their names. Snorri lists them in the *Prose Edda* as Saga, Eir, Gefjon, Fulla, Sjofn, Lofn, Var, Vor, Syn, Hlin, Snotra, and Gná. Some suggest that rather than separate beings, these handmaidens are various faces of Frigga herself. Personally, I don't think that likely, but that is the topic for another work.

Odin and Frigga have at least two children together. The first, Baldr, is the most beautiful of the gods. In *Baldrs draumar*, he has nightmares about his death, and in trying to protect her son, Frigga makes him invulnerable by asking everything in existence to promise not to hurt him. Or almost everything. She decides that mistletoe is too small and insignificant to hurt him, so she doesn't extract a promise from it. Loki discovers this and uses it to trick Frigga and Odin's other child, the blind Hodr, into using it to kill him. Nothing else is known about Hodr, but Baldr's return is prophesied to occur and usher in the new world after Ragnarok.

Thor is a son of Odin and Jord, or the earth. He is the strongest of the gods, a strength increased by a magical belt and gauntlets. Thor is also known for his hammer, Mjolnir, which he uses to protect Asgard from the Giants. Thor is called the "Protector of Man" and "Friend of Man" and is frequently seen as one of the friendlier and easier gods to work with by many heathens. Though he was made popular by Marvel Comics and then the Marvel movies, the character developed by Marvel is only loosely based on the historical accounts of Thor. I will say, though, that in my experiences Thor does seem to enjoy coffee as much as he is portrayed enjoying it in the movies. For a more in-depth analysis of Thor, I can recommend *Hammer, Oak, and Lightning* by Jeremy Baer and also published by the Troth.

Thor's wife is Sif. She is known for her long golden hair, both a sign of her beauty among the Vikings and probably a symbol for a wheat field. In one of the stories, Loki cuts her hair, and part of the reparation he has to pay is how Thor gets Mjolnir. We don't know what Sif's lineage is, although we do know she has a son, Ullr, who is as involved with winter as Skadi. We don't know who his father is, and in the surviving stories we don't see him interacting with Thor. Sif and Thor do have at least one daughter together named Thrud, which means Strength.

The second tribe of gods, the Vanir, are less well represented in the *Eddas*, although perhaps the best-known Norse goddess is one of their number. Freyja, which means Lady, is a Vanir Goddess who journeys with her father, Njord, and brother, Frey, to live in Asgard among the Æsir as hostages at the end of the war between the gods. The fact that she is listed as a hostage implies her worth within the old Norse culture.

Freyja is a goddess associated with passion, both of the sexual variety and of the sort that leads to war. She is a goddess of magic, and taught Odin the magic of seid (*seiðr*), a type of trance and spirit work. Her real name has been lost, although some think that she is Gullveig, the woman of the Vanir who was burned to death three times by the Æsir which led to the war between the tribes of gods. There are also some who think that she and Frigga are the same goddess, although the evidence on this is currently inconclusive. She is known for crying tears of amber as she searches for her missing husband. She also claims half the battle-slain, though the lore is unclear why. She is presumed to survive Ragnarok, perhaps her half of the warriors are to protect the new world. A fellow Troth Clergymember, Patricia Lafayllve, has written a book on Freyja titled *Freyja, Lady, Vanadis*, which is a wonderful resource for those wishing a more in-depth look at Freyja.

Her father, Njord, is a god of the sea, more specifically of harbors and ships. He is seen as affiliated with commerce and as such is a god of wealth. He is known for his beautiful feet, and in one of the stories we will be discussing in detail, he becomes Skadi's husband when she is given the chance to choose a spouse based only on feet.

Freyja has a brother who also accompanies Njord as a hostage. Her brother is known as Frey, although there is decent evidence that he was also known as Ing on the Continent. Skadi is Frey and Freyja's stepmother, and one of the more interesting relationships to me is that between Skadi and Frey as it shows at least casually, the relationships that form in blended families in the Viking Age.

Another important goddess in the Lore is Idunn. It is unclear which of the tribes Idunn belongs to, but she is the keeper of the apples of youth and is responsible for keeping the gods in the peak of health. As the goddess who brings about renewal, Idunn has been adopted by the Troth as their patroness, aiding in the renewal of Heathenry in the modern age. Her husband, Bragi, is the skald or poet of the gods. The kidnapping of Idunn is an important story to understanding Skadi and her family's relationship to the Æsir, as it sets up her reason for joining the tribe.

Idunn giving her apples to the gods, as envisioned by Louis Huard.
Keary and Keary, *The Heroes of Asgard* (1871).

Chapter 2: Skadi in the Lore

One common complaint of new (and not so new) Heathens is that there is so little Lore available to give us clear insights into the gods, and this is even more true for the goddesses. Regardless of how much Snorri may have changed the stories in the *Eddas* to insert a Christian influence, I for one am grateful that we have as much of the Lore as we do as other traditions are not so fortunate.

This chapter brings together the pieces of Lore that exist about Skadi and examine what they tell us about Her. Once we have a clearer picture of Skadi and her motivations, in the next chapter we will compare what we learn in *Skáldskaparmál* to the legal codes of medieval Iceland to shed light on her relationship with her father and her father's family.

Like all the *ásynjur*, or female Æsir, Skadi is in many ways a minor character in the cast of the *Eddas*, though we know significantly more about Her than many of the other deities of the Norse pantheon. Indeed, she has a leading role in several of the more significant poems, and her actions impact the lives and futures of the other gods, up to and including Ragnarok.

In the *Prose Edda*, Skadi is a character in *Skáldskaparmál* and *Gylfaginning*, the first telling of her wedding and the second of her divorce. In the *Poetic Edda*, she is mentioned in *Grímnismál*, *Hyndluljóð*, *Skírnismál*, and *Lokasenna*. Though the mentions are brief in all of these poems but *Lokasenna*, the hints they give show us her importance among her adopted Æsir. Finally, she is mentioned in *Ynglingasaga* as the bride of Odin, with whom she had sons.

The *Prose Edda*

Gylfaginning

The first poem in the *Prose Edda* to mention Skadi is *Gylfaginning*. *Gylfaginning* is the second section of the *Prose Edda*, and its title translates to "the deluding of Gylfi" who was a King of Sweden. The text is a dialogue between Gylfi and three "god-like figures" who use illusion and trickery to delude him. However, in their conversations Gylfi questions these figures, and they tell him what they know about the gods (Sturluson, *Prose Edda*, p. xv).

In Section 21 of *Gylfaginning*, Gylfi is told that Njord is the third god who lives at Nóatún (Enclosure for Ships), that he rules over the winds and can calm the sea and fire. We also learn that he was brought up in Vanaheim, but that the Vanir sent him as a hostage to the Æsir (Sturluson, *Prose Edda*, p. 33). Njord has a wife called Skadi, the daughter of Thjazi, who wanted to live in her father's home in the mountains but Njord wanted to be near the sea. They came to the agreement that they would stay nine nights in the mountains and three nights by the sea, but neither liked the other's home. Since they could not come to an agreement, Skadi returned to the mountains where she travels on skis and hunts wild animals (Sturluson, p. 34).

There are several possible interpretations for a deeper meaning behind this myth, but the one I have always favored is an explanation of the seasons. Though there is no extrapolation of this idea in the Lore, the specificity of how many nights were spent in the mountains and how many on the beach lead to a possible conclusion that their time in Thrymheim was the long cold winter of hunting season and their time in Nóatún the brief summer. Thus, we see the theme of winter married to summer. An interesting side note here is that we see a gender role reversal when compared to the Greeks. Where the Greeks had Hades bringing winter by stealing Persephone into the underworld and a male sun and female moon, the Norse myths reverse these roles (McGrath, *Njord and Skadi*, 2482).

Another point worthy of note is that when the marriage wasn't working out for her, Skadi had the option of returning to her father's lands. She did not lose her inheritance because of her marriage, and she was not forced to stay in an unhappy marriage. There is mixed evidence on how accurate a portrayal this was for women's social options in the Viking Age and how much, if at all, it carried over from goddess to human. At least the idea was there, and repeated in several stories about Freyja, that goddesses did in fact have bodily autonomy and could not be coerced. Or at least, could not be coerced without severe consequences.

Skáldskaparmál

The third section of the *Prose Edda* is titled *Skáldskaparmál*, which translates to "the language of poetry." This section includes both myths and poetry, and unlike *Gylfaginning* which was written entirely as dialogue, *Skáldskaparmál* includes both dialogue and third person storytelling (Sturluson, *Prose Edda*, p. xv).

Skadi's tale in this poem follows the story of Thjazi's theft of Idunn and her apples. Odin, Loki, and Hoenir were traveling, found a herd of oxen, and proceeded to kill one for dinner. However, they could not get the meat to cook. Thjazi, in the form of an eagle, made a bargain with them to cook their meat if they would let him eat his fill. When he proceeded to eat more than they had been expecting, the gods tried to chase Thjazi off, but when he took off, Loki was given an unexpected ride. In order to be freed, he made a bargain with Thjazi to get Idunn and her apples for the giant. Upon returning home, Loki tricked Idunn into leaving Asgard and let Thjazi carry her off. The loss of the apples made the Æsir begin to age, and so they sent Loki to retrieve her. Thjazi gave chase, and upon arriving at Asgard, was killed as he tried to breach the walls (Sturluson, *Prose Edda*, pp. 81-82).

Thjazi in eagle-shape, flying away with Loki stuck to him, as envisioned by Dorothy Hardy. Guerber, *Myths of the Norsemen* (1919).

This sets up Skadi's tale. Upon learning of her father's death, Skadi marches on Asgard with weapons of war to avenge her father. When she arrives, though, the Æsir offer her compensation rather than a fight. First, she is given a husband from among the Æsir, but she must choose him based only on seeing his feet. She was hoping to choose Baldur because he was the most beautiful, but she ended up choosing Njord instead. Then they had to make her laugh. They almost failed at this, but Loki finally managed by playing tug of war with a goat and his testicles. As a final compensation, Odin turned Thjazi's eyes into stars (Sturluson, *Prose Edda*, pp. 82-83).

This is followed by a section on Thjazi's family which tells us that Thjazi's father, Olvaldi, was very wealthy and powerful, and that Thjazi had two brothers. When their father died, they split his gold by mouthful, taking equal shares (Sturluson, *Prose Edda*, p. 83). While Snorri presumably included this section because of the explanation of a kenning it contains for gold, the implications in relation to Skadi's claiming of weregild for her father's death are enormous and will be addressed in Chapter 3.

At first glance, this tale tells how Skadi came to be numbered among the Æsir in a most amusing way (unless you're Loki or his poor testicles, or Njord who was now faced with a heavily armed wife whose dead father's eyes are watching you on your wedding night from the sky above). However, there are several things to note.

Throughout the *Eddas* there are stories of battles between the Æsir and the Giants. Skadi's father, Thjazi, is a Giant, an enemy of the Æsir, who had kidnapped one of the most powerful and important goddesses, Idunn.

So why, then, do they offer Skadi compensation rather than a fight when she shows up at their gates? Thor is well known for killing Giants who threaten Asgard. Why does he not strike her down with Mjolnir when she shows up? Why was she even allowed to get so close? While I will address why they probably gave her weregild instead of a fight in Chapter 3, that doesn't answer why she was allowed to get that close to Asgard to start with, instead of Thor meeting her with his hammer.

This story also tells us that those who were taken as hostages for good behavior were expected to assimilate into the tribe or clan of their captors. Freyja, one of the hostages exchanged at the end of the war between the gods, was treated in the other stories in the same way as the other goddesses. When giants tried to claim her for a bride, instead of being forced to accept the terms of the giants, she makes her own decisions. Not a pawn, but an autonomous goddess.

Njord, Freyja's father, is also such a prisoner. He was included in the line of gods that Skadi chose her husband from, even though he was Vanir not Æsir. In marrying him, she cemented and accepted an alliance with the Æsir, and is seen as joining their cohort. Thus, weregild paid to her remains within the tribe, and that tribe now includes Njord.

It is difficult to tell if the reason that her weregild took the form it did was because of her own nature or because of artistic license on the part of the original author of the tale. While the image of Loki playing tug-of-war with a goat is amusing even today, it certainly fit well into the bawdy style often favored and it certainly makes a lively story for a long winter night. Indeed, when I've seen this tale told to an audience, it is usually one of the humorous highpoints of the tale.

That said, there is another point to consider here, and that is the relationship that begins between Loki and Skadi in this tale. Loki was an actor in the theft of Idunn and the Apples, and the weregild being paid is due because of his actions. That he paid a painful price is logical. The one who caused the wound was expected to pay the largest portion of the weregild.

Still, the fact is that Loki had the hardest job in paying this price. Had he failed, the deal would have fallen through. This means that he is directly responsible in two ways for Skadi's inclusion among the Æsir: first because he set up the fiasco that led to her father's death, and second because he was the only one that could make her laugh.

The *Poetic Edda*

Grímnismál

The mention of Skadi in *Grímnismál* is brief. In the poem, Odin travels to the court of King Geirrod. Geirrod and his brother Agnarr had been raised by Odin and Frigg, respectively. Geirrod did not realize that the old man who arrived at his court was his foster father. He proceeded to test Odin's knowledge and to set the old man's cloak on fire and withhold food. By the time he realized what he had done and more importantly to whom, it's too late. Pulling his sword to free his foster father, Geirrod accidentally kills himself by falling on it.

However, while he's being tortured, Odin expounds upon the halls of the gods. Stanza 11 is about Thrymheim.

> Thrymheim is what a sixth hall's called.
> There that giant of all Jotuns, Thjazi, once dwelt.

But now, Skadi, glimmer-bride of the gods,
Abides there in her father's ancient hall.
(Dodds, *Poetic Edda*, p. 69)

This seems to be the basis for Snorri's statement in *Gylfaginning* that Skadi returns to her father's home (Sturluson, *Prose Edda*, p. 34).

The kenning "glimmer-bride of the gods" is particularly interesting. Bellows translates the line as "the god's fair bride" but this translation is inaccurate. The Old Icelandic is:

Þrymheimr heitir enn setti,
er Þiazi bió
sa inn amátki iotvnn;
enn nv Scaði byggvir,
scír brvðr goða,
fornar toptir fa/ðvr.

The literal translation of the line *scír brvðr goðan* is "bright bride of gods" which implies that she had more than one godly husband. The choice of the word bright is also interesting and could refer to many things. To quote

Njord and Skadi. Sander, *Edda Sämund den Vises* (1893).

Ben Waggoner, the Shope (or Publications Director) for the Troth, who has made a hobby of translating Old Icelandic stories into English for our joy:

> *Goða* is genitive plural—"of gods." The singular would be *goðs*, "of a god." "*scír brvðr goða*" is "bright bride of gods." *Skírr* means "clear; pure; bright"—and, metaphorically, "cleared of an accusation; cleansed; purified." (It's cognate with English "sheer" in the sense of "pure; complete"; if something is "sheer nonsense," that means it is pure nonsense.) Which meaning is intended here? Is Skadi "pure", or "bright", or "cleansed"? Is the word even useful at all for understanding Skadi's deep nature, or is it only there because the poet needed a word that would alliterate with the name of Skadi in the preceding half-line? Welcome to the unique joys and hassles of translation! (The Troth Facebook Group, February 23, 2019).

While he is right that we will probably never have a definitive answer to this question, I will address it more in my chapter on UPG.

Hyndluljóð

The "Lay of Hyndla" is included in some translations of the Poetic Edda, although it is preserved in its entirety in *Flateyjarbók*. In this poem, Freyja and a *völva* (seeress) named Hyndla have a conversation about Ottar's lineage (Simek, *Dictionary*, p. 169). This passage is important for understanding Skadi, because it ties her into a lineage that is shared between the Æsir and the Jotuns.

> Tallied up, there were eleven Æsir in all
> When Baldr sank into the murder-mound.
> Vali was born to avenge his brother's death –
> He slayed the hand that slayed his brother.
> This is your bloodline, Ottar the Fool.
>
> Bur's heir was Baldr's father (Odin).
> Frey wed Gerd, Gymir's daughter,
> Of the Jotuns and of Aurboda.
> Thjazi, the Jotun who hid well,
> Was their kin—his daughter was Skadi.
>   (Dodds, *Poetic Edda*, p. 259)

This recitation of lineage shows the relationships between Æsir and Jotun and sets the precedence that marriages between them were, if not common, not unheard of. Given that for most of the Asynjur we have very little information about their lineage, it is frankly impossible to determine how frequently inter-tribal marriages occurred.

What is interesting to note here is that the description seems to treat Jotuns as a clan, rather than a different type of being. While some were described as monstrous or huge, many were seen as lovely and certainly capable of mating with the gods. Is this the viewpoint of multiple writers and sources? Or are there more complex social structures among Jotunkind than are elucidated in the lore?

We know from many of the Eddic poems that the Jotuns have powerful magic that is in some cases more than a match for the Æsir. We learned in *Skáldskaparmál* that Thjazi, Skadi's father, was one of them. He was able to use his magic to get the best of Odin, Hoenir, and Loki combined. Odin and Loki are arguably two of the more magically powerful Æsir though little is known about Hoenir. That Thjazi managed to keep them from cooking their dinner by controlling the fire (or shielding it, it is unclear just what he did), in the form of an eagle powerful enough to carry Loki off through the air, then demand Loki kidnap Idunna in order for Thjazi to return him to his companions indicates that he was the more powerful being.

Skírnismál

In *Skírnismál*, Frey sits on Hlidskjalf, Odin's high seat that allows him to see into all the realms, glimpses Gerd, and falls immediately in love with her. Skadi sends Skirnir, Frey's page, to talk to him and see what is wrong with him.

> Skirnir, arise and go
> Ask our son to talk,
> Find out who's enflamed
> Our kin's lush brain.
>   (Dodds, *Poetic Edda*, p. 76)

There are two interesting things to consider out of this passage. First, although she is not Frey's mother, she takes on the role of caring about him and calls him son and kin. We do not know where in the marriage/divorce cycle this poem falls for Skadi and Njord. In the end, it does not seem to matter. He became family either through her marriage to Njord or through their mutual adoption by the Æsir. If she had only called him "kin" then the latter would make more sense. But she does not. She calls him "our son" implying that, in marrying his father, he became her son and regardless of how her relationship to Njord changed, the stepmother bond did not change. This gives us a brief glimpse into blended families of the time. Indeed, the concept of family at the time was significantly different from the modern concept of a nuclear family (Miller, "Some Aspects of Householding," pp. 321-324). Fostering children to cement bonds was not uncommon and had little or no basis in blood. Even so, fostering made one a sort of family as was the relationship between Odin and Geirrod noted above. It is this sort of bond we most likely see between Skadi and Frey. Particularly since she likely does not have sons of her own at this time.

Interestingly, we do not see similar familial interactions between Skadi and Freyja. There is no place where she seems to take on the role of Mother to the other goddess, at least not among the lore that survives. Possibly this is because the relationship between mother and step-daughter was different than that between mother and step-son. Perhaps it is because of the specific relationship between these two goddesses as, in many ways, opposites. For if Skadi is a goddess of winter and cold harsh mountains, Freyja is the complete opposite in my experiences with her. Her hall and home are bright and warm, and to me Freyja is the embodiment of the lushness of the ripening spring into summer.

Second, we learned in *Hyndluljóð* that Skadi and Gerd are not only both Jotuns, but they are kin. Frey knew whose house he was looking into, as he calls Gymir by name. The question then becomes whether part of his despair in seeing Gerd was because of the kin relationships between his love and his stepmother and the potential impact it would have on his prospects with her.

In pagan times, there was a simple definition of incest which banned sexual relationships among immediate, nuclear family members. However, beginning in the late ninth century and lasting until the Fourth Lateran Council in 1215, the church added active prohibitions against those related by blood (consanguinity), related by marriage (affinity), or related by the sacraments (such as through godparenting) (Jochens, *Women in Old Norse Society*, p. 42). Based on these laws and the date of the poem's authorship, some of Frey's lamenting could be based on the impossible situation of his stepmother's relationship to his beloved. Snorri, as a religious man and lawyer, would certainly have been familiar with these legal codes even if he lived after the Fourth Lateran Council. Indeed, some of Gerd's reluctance to marry Frey could very well have also been motivated by this understanding of who was and was not an acceptable spouse.

Some would argue that different rules applied to gods than to humans. There are plenty of cases in mythology, both Norse and other, that depict incestuous marriages within complicated family trees. And given the insults thrown at Frey and Freyja by Loki in the *Lokasenna*, it is doubtful that the siblings in particular are strangers to incest. Marriage to a cousin-by-marriage wouldn't stop a god, but the relationship still bears noting.

Lokasenna

The final installment of Skadi's representation in the Poetic Edda comes in the *Lokasenna*, or Loki's Flyting. In his introductory material, Hollander states that there is no reason to implicitly believe Loki's claims against the gods (Hollander, *Poetic Edda*, p. 90). Though *Lokasenna* does not specifically state that Loki is bound because of his part in Baldr's death, this poem does set up the conditions that lead to Ragnarok.

In Loki's exchange with Skadi, she threatens him with captivity while bound in his sons' guts, which is when he admits his part in her father's death, "I'll first have had the foremost hand among the hands slaying Thjazi," to which she threatens cold council from her shrines and sanctums (Dodds, *Poetic Edda*, p. 104). He follows this with claiming that she slept with him, although by this point, he has made this claim of most of the Ásynjur and it carries very little weight.

The final paragraph of the poem gives Loki's final disposition. As predicted, he is bound to a rock by his sons' guts, and Skadi provides the final punishment, hanging a venomous snake over him to constantly drip burning venom into his face (Dodds, *Poetic Edda*, p. 107). This seems particularly harsh, given their interactions in *Skáldskaparmál*, where Loki was the only god who could make her laugh, and that through his own physical pain.

While I will discuss the problems with her enacting further punishment on Loki for the death of her father in the section on Skadi as Ring-Lady, I think it is important to discuss her statement about having shrines and sanctums. There is evidence in both Sweden and to a lesser extent Norway that places were named for Skadi. *Skadavi, Skedvi,* and *Skea* are all place names derived from *Skaðavé*, "Skadi's sacred place," and may well be evidence of cultic practice to her (Simek, *Dictionary*, p. 287).

Further worth noting in this section, Skadi is the only goddess who defends herself against Loki's accusations. The others ignore or deflect them. She threatens him back. It could be nothing, but it could also be a testament to her nature, even at this point, as the headstrong woman who marched alone against the abode of the gods.

Ynglinga Saga

The final mention of Skadi in the Lore is found in *Ynglinga Saga*. Though the verse is known best because of Snorri's inclusion of it in *Heimskringla*, the original verse is credited to Eyvindr Finnsson skáldaspillir in his poem *Háleygjatal*. Eyvindr was born in approximately 915 CE and died in 990 CE. This particular text seems to have been written circa 985. His maternal grandmother was a daughter of Harold Fair-Hair, and he seems to have been close to Harold's son Hakon the Good. Eyvindr has been called the last important Norwegian skald (Poole, "Eyvindr skáldaspillir"). The original verse as penned by Eyvindr is:

> *Þann skjaldblætr*
> *skattfæri gat*
> *Ása niðr*
> *við járnviðju,*
> *þás þau mær*
> *í manheimum*
> *skatna vinr*
> *ok Skaði byggðu,*
> *sævar beins,*
> *ok sunu marga*
> *ǫndurdís*
> *við Óðni gat.*

Which translates as:

> járgr] with the female from Járnviðr, when those renowned ones, the friend of warriors [= Óðinn] and Skaði [giantess], lived in the lands of the maiden of the bone of the sea [(*lit.* 'maiden-lands of the bone

of the sea') ROCK > GIANTESS > = Jǫtunheimar 'Giant-lands'], and the ski-goddess [= Skaði] bore many sons with Óðinn (Poole, "Eyvindr skáldaspillir").

Erling Momsen's translation is a bit easier to read:

> Njord took a wife called Skadi; she would not live with him and afterwards gave herself to Odin. They got many sons and one of them was called Saeming. About him Eyving Scaldaspiller has made this:
>
> Hail, lord!
> The chief was begotten
> By the kin of the god
> With the giantess,
> In those days of old
> When the prince's friend
> Was Skadi's mate
> In the Manheims,
> And the fell-sliding
> Ski-goddess
> Begot with Odin
> Many sons.
> (Sturlason, *Heimskringla*, p. 6)

There are two things about this entry of interest. First, that it gives another mention of Snorri's earlier work depicting the divorce between Skadi and Njord which we saw in *Gylfaginning*. One possible reason to mention the divorce here was to clarify that she was in fact divorced without children to Njord, thus reaffirming Saeming's father as Odin.

More importantly, though, is the second point, which is that rarely in the sagas do we have much discussion of a maternal line (Jochens 13). The fact that Snorri includes Skadi in Saeming's lineage at all gives weight to her as a female to be reckoned with rather than merely a vessel for procreation.

Chapter 3: Social Norms

Skadi the Ring-Lady

Skadi is an interesting character among the Æsir with many lessons to teach modern Heathens. Though she is not the only jotun to marry into the tribe of the Æsir, the circumstances surrounding her joining the gods in Asgard are unique. Independent and fearless, she is nevertheless committed to her family, their honor, and their future. However, part of what makes her story so unique is its juxtaposition against the social norms of Iceland around the behavior of women and their legal status, particularly in the post-conversion period in which Snorri is writing.

The laws of early Iceland spelled out very clearly how weregild should be collected: who was eligible to receive it and how much of it was to be paid. Weregild was paid by the clan, not an individual, and as such, everyone was expected to pay into the amount owed the clan of a murdered man (or woman) depending on their relationship to the killer. Likewise, the clan who had suffered the murder had clearly delineated expectations of who was to receive weregild.

Under Icelandic law, there were four rings of payers and receivers. The first ring was the largest, the fourth the smallest. The first ring was paid and received by the father, son, and brother. The second was paid and received by the father's father, the son's son, the mother's father, and the daughter's son. The third ring consisted of the father's brother, brother's son, mother's brother, and sister's son. The final ring was distributed among male first cousins (Dennis, *Grágás*, location 4627).

There was only one time a woman was expected to either pay into or collect weregild: if she is the "daughter of the dead man and no proper receiver of the main ring otherwise exists but atonement payers are alive." Then she takes the same share as a son, although only if she is unmarried (Dennis, *Grágás*, location 4770).

There is no mention in the Lore that Skadi had any siblings, much less a brother to claim Thjazi's weregild. That said, we do know from *Skáldskaparmál* that Thjazi had two brothers; Idi and Gang (Sturluson, *Prose Edda*, p. 83). As brothers, they should have been eligible to claim the primary ring of weregild. Further, we know that his brothers were quite interested in inheritance and gold: after all, their splitting of their father's estate gave rise to a kenning for gold. Why then, was Skadi left to march on Asgard alone to claim her father's weregild? Were her uncles cowards? Or dead? Was she the only one left?

Logic would presume they were dead. We learn from *Grímnismál* that Skadi inherits Thjazi's lands and later returns to Thrymheim (Dodds, *Poetic Edda*, p. 69). Were her uncles still living, they would have been the primary heirs of their brother, but this does not answer the question about the rest of the Clan. We know Gerd was Skadi's kin. Skadi had uncles. She must have had male cousins, too, right? Where was the rest of the Clan? And why did Skadi do what no one else would? Why did She take on the Æsir? Alone?

There is another extension of this law that comes into play in *Skáldskaparmál*. By accepting a husband, Skadi in effect signs a quit claim on any future payments for her father's death, relinquishing any further claim to either revenge or recompense for her loss. This is in part because she was given as weregild, but also because once she is married she has no further legal ground to claim it. In this regard, she breaks the agreement when she

Skadi chooses a husband. Klugh, *Tales from the Far North* (1909).

threatens Loki in *Lokasenna*. The gild has already been paid and accepted for Thjazi's death by the clan of the Æsir. Also, legally only one person can be named as a killer under the oldest Icelandic law, as recorded in the manuscript *Grágas*. Technically, the killer was whoever caught Thjazi on fire as he flew over the wall, which was not Loki, as he was still being chased and carrying Idunn. Further, it could be argued that Loki had already paid his share of the weregild by his game of tug of war with a goat, finally getting Skadi to laugh.

In the complex family relationships among the gods, Skadi's punishment of Loki seemingly makes no sense. It cannot be for his role in killing Thjazi, and it is unlikely because of him claiming she'd invited him to her bed. It makes most sense to think it was over Baldr's death, even if she had not married Baldr as she'd once wished. Given that she does marry Odin and have children with him, and given that the stories of the Lore exist outside of time, it could be that she is avenging him as his future stepmother and mother of his half-siblings, although while this is certainly in character for her, it is unusual under the laws of Iceland.

As in other places in the Lore, this could have been written simply because, like the idea of playing tug of war with your balls and a goat, it makes for a memorable story. Personally, though, I think it's more than that. I think it tells us more about Skadi's inherent nature, and I'll discuss it more in the chapter on UPG.

Gender Roles

Skadi's pursuit of weregild is not the only way in which she challenges gender roles in the Lore. In truth, there is nowhere in the lore where she is shown taking on traditional female roles, aside from having Odin's children. She is not known for her spinning, or for serving mead. Instead, she hunts, she has weapons of war, and she punishes those who would hurt her kin. All of this crosses boundaries that are rarely crossed in the Lore or elsewhere, and Skadi does it with ease and unselfconsciously.

According to Jochens, marriage in pagan Iceland was negotiated between the bride's father and the groom or the groom's father (*Women in Old Norse Society*, p. 25). Indeed, a woman's consent was not needed to make a marriage binding; consent was something introduced by Christian priests post-Conversion (Jochens, p. 37). In this regard, both Skadi's marriage to

Njord and her marriage to Odin are unusual. What makes this even more unusual is Njord's passive acceptance of his wedding (McGrath, *Njord and Skadi*, location 4357). This is a distinct change in gender roles and could be seen not only as further evidence that Njord was originally the female Nerthus, but also evidence that Skadi was originally male, based on word declensions (Turville-Petre, *Myth and Religion*, p. 165). I am not a linguist, nor do I play one on television. I do not have the capacity to debate the merits of this argument, or if and when our gods changed their genders. If that's something you wish to pursue, you should take it up with Turville-Petre and the gods themselves.

Male and female hunters on skis in northern Scandinavia. These are Saami people. Saami women hunted and worked outdoors, and it is thought by some that the Norse conception of Skadi is based on a Saami woman. Illustration from Olaus Magnus, *Historia de gentibus septentrionalibus* (1555).

Chapter 4: UPG

For those unfamiliar with the concept, UPG stands for Unverified Personal Gnosis. It can range from something that is clearly linked to the Lore to something that is wildly improbable based on the Lore. Some of it is quite lighthearted. Some of it is an attempt to "modernize" our gods and goddesses, reimagining them in this modern era and how they have grown and changed over the last thousand or so years.

Because of this, UPG falls along a gradient for me. Some of it is a clear extrapolation from existing Lore and doesn't require much consideration. It's a logical conclusion, even if it requires a small intuitive leap. For example, it is well documented in the Lore that many of the giants have powerful magic, strong enough to confound the gods. Therefore, even though it is not expressly stated in any of the surviving stories, it is not a huge leap in logic to accept that Skadi also possesses some magical abilities.

Then there is the UPG that has no basis in Lore, but is a fairly minor thing, often a small embellishment, that makes stories come to life. Especially stories set in the modern era as people take to retelling, updating, or creating new stories for our gods and goddesses. An example of this is, as I mentioned above, that Thor likes coffee. I've heard from several people that Thor does seem to like coffee. It's my experience that coffee is well received as an offering to Thor. But at the end of the day, it doesn't really impact his character or essential Thor-ness if he does or not. Another example of this is the idea that today Thor would drive a Dodge Ram pickup truck (because goats, now rams. . .). Or the way that in a fictional book Diana Paxson named Freyja's cats Beegold and Treegold, and now people quote it like it is fact. It's not in the Lore. It's probably not an important detail, but it does provide flesh to the skeleton.

Then there's the UPG that, well, that's a stretch. Things like the gods are actually aliens from another dimension that created earth to provide a mining colony for a rare isotope that powers their intergalactic travel. I mean, it's within the realm of possibility. . . but. . . .

I am not interested in judging other people's UPG. In fact, I even spent quite a bit of time trying to decide whether I wanted to include a UPG section in this book. In the end, I chose to do so because I think it's important to share our experiences that go beyond the Lore as we build a modern practice.

I also think it is critical that such things are labeled as UPG.

Therefore, what I am sharing with you in this section are the insights and ideas and inspirations I have had working with Skadi over the last eight years. I make no claim that they are real, accurate, or universally useful.

If they help you, great. If not, feel free to disregard them.

Health

Skadi first came to me when I was suffering from an injury, depressed, and rapidly gaining weight because of the first two. I was stuck, that's really the only word for it, and she encouraged me to get myself Unstuck. When I asked her how to do that, what would be the first step, her response was very clearly to get a handle on my health.

I want to be clear that I don't say that to weight-shame anyone. I'm not a small woman by any stretch of the imagination. Her imperative to me had nothing to do with size and everything to do with two things: health and stamina.

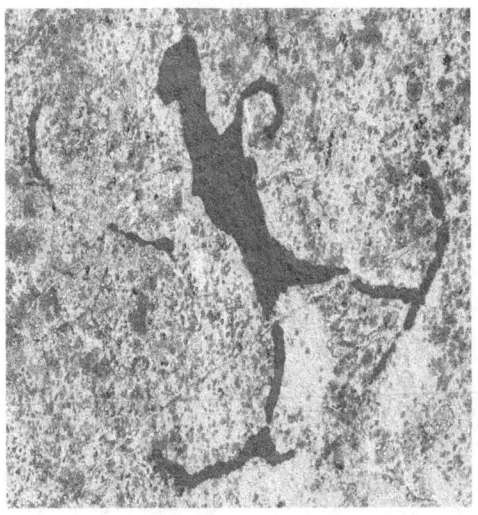

Skadi wants those she chooses, or who choose her, to treat their bodies as both a temple and a weapon. She wants you to be in your best possible physical health, and she's happy to motivate you to get there. Skadi is at home in the mountains, in the cold, in a brutal climate. The Lore makes that very clear. In order to survive there, much less thrive, you have to be able to face the challenges of her home.

For me, I took up running and hiking. I choose to seek her in the wild places she favors, and push myself in order to be able to get there.

Stone Age rock art from Alta, Norway, showing a skier. Unknown photographer. Courtesy of Wikimedia Commons, CC BY-SA 3.0.

But it was about a lot more than weight. It was also about getting myself the medical care I had been putting off so that I could be my best self. It included seeing a therapist and working through my emotional issues that came from several miscarriages and a failed marriage.

If you want to work with Skadi, you have to be willing to put in the work to be the healthiest you that you can possibly be.

People do this in different ways. People start in different places. People have different needs. For some, like myself, it was a combination of getting the proper medical care and medications and doing what we all KNOW we need to do and get more exercise. For others, it might be eating healthier and honoring themselves with their food choices. Skadi is a huntress. She is known for her hunting in the Lore. There is a difference between "dieting" and eating healthful food. Skadi would never encourage the first, because "dieting" is generally done for the wrong reasons. Most people "diet" to better fit to social pressures around appearance. Skadi couldn't care less about that. But getting a healthy diet that meets your nutritional needs and honors the animals you consume, yes, that is a core component of honoring and growing closer to Her.

If you wish to work with Skadi, no matter how fit you currently are, be prepared to push yourself. No matter how good we take care of ourselves, this is an area where there is always room for improvement, and she will demand that you improve.

Goddess of the Hunt

Although she is never explicitly called a goddess of the hunt in the lore, in my interactions with her hunting is a central theme. Hunting has two purposes: food and protection. Skadi engages in both.

Hunting for food was an important part of life in every era of the pre-modern age. Wild game provided sustenance, leather, fur, and any number of other useful bits. In many cultures, the first kill is a critical rite of passage. In my interactions with her, Skadi is a goddess who provides for her people. One way that she does this is in through hunting, literally putting the meat on the table.

Over the years, she has encouraged me to take up hunting myself, although I have yet to do so. Her interest is in having me better understand what life was like for our forebears, and also that I learn to be more self-reliant. However, time has never permitted it for me. I work a full-time job as it is, in addition to my writing and other religious obligations, and family life. I live in an urban environment where hunting is not an everyday activity. My sustenance is provided by a paycheck, not my skills with a bow and arrow. That said, if you are a hunter, or are interested in becoming one, I would encourage you to work with her in this aspect.

There is also the idea of hunting for protection. There are predators out there that must be slain in order to protect the folk you are responsible for protecting. In times past, that was often a literal hunt. Whether it was a bear or wolf driven by winter hunger to attack villages, or an escaped boar with no fear of people, there were real dangers in the forest that had to be dealt with.

In this modern age, humans have a different relationship with wildlife, at least here in the northern part of the US where I live. While there are some dangerous predators remaining, their numbers are small due to their systemic extermination (gators down in Florida are a whole other matter as far as I'm concerned, and one of many reasons I live where the air hurts my face).

But just because there isn't a danger from wildlife, that doesn't mean that there aren't dangerous things out there that need thinning. In my experience, Skadi has been very hands on in her willingness to teach me these skills. For example, the skills of patience and perseverance are critical for

Stone Age rock art from Bergbukten B, Alta, Norway, showing hunter and reindeer. Photo by Hans A. Rosbach. Courtesy of Wikimedia Commons, CC BY-SA 3.0.

a hunter of wild game—but **also** for a hunter of a new job, or a house, or many other things we "hunt" in the modern era.

Personality: Cold, Logical and Warrior Trained

As I stated in the Lore section, Skadi was willing to gird her loins and march on Asgard when her male relatives were either afraid or dead. Skadi must have had some experience with weapons of war beyond the bow she used for hunting before she went on this mission. While not explicitly stated in the lore, in my experience, her interactions are very logical. She considers her options, then makes the best choice available to her. Whether it's choosing her husband, or choosing her fate, she faces her future with the inner will that defines a warrior. Warriors, after all, are allowed to be afraid. It isn't the absence of fear that defines a warrior. Bravery, instead, is acting in the face of that fear, and that is what Skadi does and what she would have her followers do as well.

Some people experience this as emotionally cold, but I do not. She isn't emotionally cold at all. Quite the opposite. She is very invested in her followers. But she is a logical tactician, and if a hard decision is to be made, she doesn't shy away from it. She faced her fears, she expects her followers to as well.

Skadi is a not a goddess who accepts excuses. She puts honor first, her own and that of those she considers kin. If you promise her something, you'd best make sure it's a priority for you because she does exact her price. And if you act without honor around her, she doesn't give second chances.

The best word for this is Integrity. Integrity is not what most people think it is. Integrity is doing what you say you're going to do. Period. Keeping your oaths and promises. And if circumstances arise that keep you from doing so, which let's be honest does in fact happen, it is about paying your *schild* and making new arrangements with honor. Not excuses, but making it right. Not hiding out and avoiding your responsibilities, but showing up and fixing whatever it was you messed up on. The heart of integrity is honoring your word as your bond.

Her Family

As I mentioned in the section on weregild and the section on her relationship with Frey and Gerd, family is everything to Skadi, and her Clan among the Jotuns is large. She has many relatives who, for their own reasons, didn't want to stir up a fight with the Æsir over one of their members who had clearly been in the wrong, and so they let her march alone on Asgard and, when she left Njord, keep her inheritance intact.

I do think her uncles were dead. They were too greedy for gold to have let her keep Thrymheim otherwise. And she may or may not have other close cousins. But even if she doesn't have immediate male family, she does have a large Clan that exist across the world: wherever there are high, snow-capped mountains, she has kin. And there isn't a continent on Earth that doesn't have those snowy peaks.

If, as many say, Jotuns are the nature spirits that our ancestors feared because of their power over the elements of the natural world, then her Clan becomes even larger. After all, there are a lot more mountains that lose their snowcaps in the summer. And if Gerd is her cousin, as Snorri hints, then Skadi has kin among the earth giants as well as the frost giants, the kindly ones who embody the earth around us.

Relationship with Ullr

Franz Schröder suggested in 1941 that Skadi was related to the god Ullr, who also hunted and traveled on skis, said to be the son of Sif. He compared them to the Vanic deities Freyr and Freyja, and to the Finnish deities of hunting and the forest, Tapio and Mielikki, who were often seen as a couple. He suggested that Ullr and Skadi were siblings and also lovers (*Skadi und die Götter Skandinaviens*, pp. 109-116).

Archer on skis, possibly Ullr, depicted on the Böksta Runestone, near Balingsta, Uppland, Sweden.

Scholars have pointed out that 1) we don't know who Ullr's father is; 2) we don't know anything about Sif's lineage, but we assume she is some variation of a fertility deity given that her hair was probably analogous to wheat which means that, like Gerd, she was probably some variation of an earth giant; 3) Skadi and Ullr share pretty much all of the same characteristics, including hunting, skiing, archery, etc.; and 4) Thjazi has a desire for fertility goddesses among the Æsir (see the myth of the Theft of Idunn). If Ullr and Skadi are siblings, Thjazi presumably, either consensually or through abduction and rape, fathered Ullr on Sif before her marriage to Thor.

I'm not convinced that I'm willing to go quite this far. This certainly goes into the realms of extreme UPG, even if there are certain logical conclusions based on the Lore that play a part in it.

I am, however, convinced that Skadi and Ullr were related in some way, even if it is to the same level that Skadi and Gerd were related, where Sif, like Gerd, is a goddess of cultivated land and Ullr, as her son, is the offspring of a giantess. Specifics on this have yet to be revealed to me, if they ever are.

That said, there have been a couple of times Ullr has shown up in my trance work around Thrymheim, and if not siblings, they are at least cousins and friends.

Skadi and Gender Fluidity

As I mentioned in the section on gender roles, there are linguistic arguments as to whether Njord was originally Nerthus and Skadi was male based on declensions of language. I am not a linguist, and Skadi has never appeared in a male form to me, and I don't have a particularly close relationship with Njord.

What I will say, adamantly, is that Skadi doesn't give even half a dead rat's derriere whether someone who comes to her is male, female, non-binary, or gender-fluid so long as they're honorable. Likewise, she doesn't care who you're sleeping with or what arrangements you make, so long as you approach your partners with honesty and honor.

The Bright Bride of Gods

As mentioned in the Lore section, Skadi is referred to as the Bright Bride of Gods in *Heimskringla*, and it is unclear if this is a good translation of "bright" or if the meaning was more along the lines of "purified."

In truth, it could be either or both.

However, this is a section on UPG, so I am sharing mine.

Depiction of a Saami bride being led to her wedding. Schefferus, *Lapponia* (1673)

In my work with Skadi, she appears as a tall goddess, one who towers over most of those around her. Her muscles are defined and solid as the granite of the mountains. Her skin is very pale, her eyes the bright blue of ice, and her hair shimmering snow white. Not the golden wheat color that was so prized among the Norse, but the shimmering white of fresh snow so pure that it can cause snow blindness.

It is this last, the brightness that can hurt you if you don't take proper precautions, that Skadi embodies.

The Venomous Snake

One place in the lore her unwillingness to forgive is at its clearest is in her interactions with Loki. While I think their relationship is complicated, she has been very clear with me her thoughts on Loki and the role he played in her father's death.

When I've mentioned this in the past to friends, they pointed out that without Loki, she would never have joined the Æsir, that they have been friends. And I don't deny that this is true. I have no doubt that they are in fact related, given that both are born of the Giant Clan. That may well have been a part of the reason that Loki was able to get her to laugh: as a fellow Giant, he understood her sense of humor better than the Æsir did.

But if that's the case, then his taking the foremost hand in killing her father makes the crime even greater, as it would have constituted kinslaying, one of the few things seen as unforgivable in the Viking law codes, as the weregild would have been owed to the same family and no restitution could ever have truly been made.

My friend, Melissa Hill, pointed out to me that Loki and Skadi have opposite natures. Most people see him as some variation of a fire-god, and he is frequently depicted with flames, or red hair or eyes (or both) to show this aspect of him. He is the unpredictable fire that can burn out of control, or the fires of Ragnarok that will destroy the world. Most of my Lokean friends agree that his nature is that of fire, and the simplest shrines to him usually includes a candle. Skadi, on the other hand, is an ice-goddess. Melissa asked me what would be the most logical form for poison to take for a fire-god? An icicle. In her UPG, the serpent is in fact an icicle that melts slowly and drips into the fire, which makes it sputter and causes it pain. There is a certain logic to this, and while I'm not completely convinced, I decided to include it here for other people to ponder, too.

Her Magical Nature

There is nowhere in the Lore where Skadi is mentioned for being magical, apart from hanging the venomous serpent over Loki (because that almost had to have been conjured whether actual snake or icicle). She isn't shown as having a magic cloak like Freyja, or a magical ship like Baldur. She isn't generally associated with magic of any kind (other than maybe hunting luck).

I don't know whether this is an oversight on the part of Snorri, or a part of the traditions we've lost to time and fire and sunken ships, but my experience with her is quite the opposite. And while I cannot point out a place in the lore where her magic is spoken of, I can and will point out that, as stated in the section on *Skáldskaparmál,* her father had magic to rival Odin and Loki together. Thus, I would argue that while it is ENTIRELY my UPG, it isn't outside the realm of logic that Skadi has magical abilities of her own. She has certainly shown herself to me as a magically inclined goddess.

Though I have never witnessed the full extent of her magic, what I have seen tends to fall in the categories of hunting and tracking, of finding the trail that I thought had been lost, or of facing odds that are against you and coming out on top.

Fylgia Magic

Sometimes it is easier to ask someone else to write a short essay than to try and paraphrase for them. Such is the essay that follows here by my partner in life and magic. As part of his practice, he has worked extensively with Skadi in the aspect of Fetch magic. My own experiences mirror his to some extent.

In short, though, one of the areas of magic she is particularly fond of is fetch magic. Like her father, Skadi is a shapeshifter. Thjazi transformed into an eagle on more than one occasion. I have seen Skadi take multiple forms, whichever is best suited to the occasion: eagle or owl, fox or wolf, and bear are among her favorites depending on how far she wishes to travel or what she wishes to hunt. Different animals have different strengths to bring to the work she wishes to accomplish.

She has had two primary lessons for me when it comes to fetch work. First, that my family has certain allies that are easier for me to find within myself. Among the Norse, this was called the *fylgja,* similar to the fetch in Irish folklore. The fylgja is a spirit that accompanies a person and is frequently associated with a familial line. The second, that like everything else, magic is a muscle that must be conditioned. This skill, in particular, doesn't always come easily.

Fetch Magic, by Jeremy Baer

The subject of berserkers and "shapeshifting" has been written about at length. Within the Troth's own Lore Program you can find papers on the topic (cf. "Odin's Own: Berserkers as the All-Father's Instruments" by myself, and "It's Hamr Time: A Survey of Magical Terminology in Egil's Saga" by Thomas De Mayo). Let me simply recap the very basics for purposes of the following essay.

Berserkers were warriors who displayed the characteristics of wolves or bears. They were often described as having great strength and size and were usually thought to be impervious to fire and steel. They were seemingly connected to Odin through his mastery of *seiðr*.

A related but broader concept is the subject of shapeshifting. The Heathen soul was thought to be multivalent, with various interlocking parts. Different parts had different functions, and the skilled esoteric worker could manipulate these parts to conduct magic. Within this type of "soul magic" it was thought one had a type of animal double who conveyed certain characteristics to the individual. This animal double could also be projected to engage in combat or perform reconnaissance on foes. To what extent shapeshifting and *seiðr* is synonymous is matter of debate, but it is this author's opinion that shapeshifting was a central aspect of *seiðr*. Outside of Heathenry, in various native traditions, there is a wider lore of soul-magic and animal shapeshifting that one can peruse for erudition.

My work with Skadi has involved an element of fetch magic, the "fetch" or *fylgja* being a term for an animal-like double that either accompanies the individual through life, or is itself part of the complicated corpus of an individual's soul parts. My UPG, as discussed elsewhere, is that Skadi is imbued with magic, as much as Giants elsewhere generally seem to be magical beings, even if the Lore doesn't specifically enumerate magic as part of her skillsets. It is further UPG that her tryst with Odin and the sons she produced can be esoterically tied to Berserkers, Odin's ecstatic warriors. Tying this all together, I believe Skadi as Lady of the Mountains and Mistress of the Hunt helps empower the fetch of her devotees.

Working with one's fetch is an extensive issue that lays outside the scope of this essay. In any case, such work can be extremely personal, the details of which are not necessarily to be penned for mass publication. However,

Snow has elsewhere written some trance inductions to meet Skadi which can be readily used. I would suggest to the querent that if one were to meet Skadi in her mountain hall, if one travels there with an air of respect and exploration, Skadi can reveal to the querent how best to employ one's fetch.

The physical and mental strength that the giantess demands is not only a matter of physical being; it carries over to some degree in esoteric realms as well. It's harder to manifest a strong or fast fetch if oneself is physically weak or slow. Mind, body and spirit all seem to be highly connected on some level, and Skadi demands all be finely tuned for the hunt.

Mother of the Berserkers

As Jeremy mentioned in his essay about Fetch Magic, one of the areas of UPG we have both experienced about Skadi has been that she had her own reasons for agreeing to be Odin's bride and mothering a line of warriors—that there was a reason Snorri spent time in *Heimskringla* adding Skadi and her lineage to the story of Saeming. I want to give the caveat that this is UPG. Beyond the lines in *Heimskringla* that they had many sons, there is no mention of their family together. Like all UPG, take it with a grain of salt. But if it empowers your magical practice, then we're glad.

If Odin is the master of *seiðr*, having learned it from Freyja, Skadi is the mistress of wild things. Odin may be seen as a god of war by many, but in the sense of the broader strategy. Patron of princes and skalds, yes. Why are the Berserkers so closely tied to him? One would think Thor would be a better patron for the shock troops. The answer is mostly found in the way that the Berserkers fought, with a battle frenzy driven by divine madness. He gives the frenzy, but it is through a union with Skadi that the Berserkers find the physical stamina and prowess, through her gifts as a giantess, daughter of a master shapeshifter and shapeshifter herself, that they receive the gift of their animal selves.

Jeremy has written about his perspective on this, as well, and so I shall share it here with you. While I may disagree with my husband on some of the finer points (such as what women find appealing or what Skadi got out of the bargain), there is an artistry in this idea that makes a fair amount of sense when considered from the convergence of logic and magic.

Skadi and Odin, by Jeremy Baer

In *Ynglingasaga* we are told a different account of Skadi than the more well-known story relayed in Sturluson's *Prose Edda*. Skadi married Njord but did not consummate the marriage in sexual terms. Later, she marries Odin (here euhemerized into a powerful priest-sorcerer rather than a god). The two have many sons. These few brief sentences are told within the context of Odin's story, where Skadi figures as but one of Odin's various adventures.

Let us for a moment assume the myth contains some kind of spiritual truth. This tryst between Odin and Skadi raises some interesting questions. Why did Skadi choose to reproduce with Odin whereas she refused the attentions of Njord? What was it that Odin offered that Njord didn't?

To answer those questions, perhaps we should step back a second and contemplate the natures of both beings. Let us do so with full respect to the wide range of lore, rather than what is merely presented in *Ynglingasaga*.

Odin is the master magician of the Æsir and one of the wisest beings in the Nine Worlds. He gave one of his eyes at Mimir's well for wisdom. He hung on Yggdrasil for nine nights, an act of "shamanic" sacrifice to discover the runes, and subsequently mastered eighteen runic spells. He learned the "womanly" art of *seiðr* from Freyja. He is a wanderer and a deceiver, and he boasts to his son Thor regarding his prowess with women. He presides over kings, aristocrats and heroes, and he leads the Einherjar to the fateful battle at Ragnarok.

Skadi is a giantess, daughter of Thjazi. The giants have a complicated relationship with the Æsir. They are the elder beings from whom the gods are descended and are renowned for their wisdom and magic. And yet they have shifting relations with the Æsir, sometimes friendly, sometimes antagonistic, the latter usually ending up on the business end of Thor's hammer. Skadi herself, mistress of mountains and snow, was willing to march on all of Asgard (and presumably die in the process) to avenge her father. Ultimately, however, she was reconciled to them, becoming their ally.

In Skadi and Odin two different currents meet. We find a representative of an elder race (Skadi) meeting a younger one (Odin). We find a force representing bravery, familial ties, the winter land and rightful vengeance (Skadi) meeting a force representing wisdom, wandering, deceit and war (Odin).

Odin is the master magician, having discovered runes and having learned *seiðr*. While Skadi is not presented in the lore as casting magic, all her people are known for that trait. We must presume she herself had some affinity for magic not expressed in the lore (after all, how did she expect to confront all of Asgard by physical might alone? She must have had a few esoteric tricks up her sleeve).

What did Skadi see in Odin? The All-Father is certainly powerful, and power is often a compelling aphrodisiac to women. But more so, Odin as master of disguises and god of galdor could charm and beguile his way into many a maiden's bed. Perhaps Skadi was not immune to these charms.

What did Odin see in Skadi? Just another sexual conquest? Perhaps. However, it's been my impression that Odin prefers to conquer strong, feisty females. Skadi is nothing if not strong.

Further, Odin usually has a strategic imperative underlying his actions. If we return for a moment to the comparative natures of Skadi and Odin, we might guess what Odin wanted: strong sons. The physical strength and primal magic of Skadi's line when blended with Odinic wisdom and magic would make for powerful offspring indeed—apt soldiers for Odin's use. Skadi in return becomes proud matriarch to a line of powerful warriors.

To take this a step further into the wanton realm of UPG, what if these offspring were warriors of mighty stature, whose magic harnessed the primal currents of nature as represented by Skadi? The ultimate origins of the Berserkers are a matter of some debate. My wife and I would like to suggest this union of Skadi and Odin may, at least on an esoteric and mythic level, help fill in some of those blanks.

And thus it was no accident that I, who call Odin as patron, eventually bumped into Skadi, though before meeting my wife I honestly had no interest in the giantess whatsoever. . .

Njord and Skadi, as envisioned by Wägner and MacDowell, *Asgard and the Gods* (1886).

Chapter 5: Poetry, Prayers, Journeys, and Rituals

Skadi has been very clear with me that those who call on her for aid should first establish a relationship with her. Thus, this section has been very specifically ordered into Poems and Prayers, Journeys, and Rituals.

Begin to build your relationship with prayers, perhaps setting up a small altar to her. Pour or share a drink with her (UPG: she likes vodka) and make a few offerings, including the offerings of prayers. Spend some time thinking about her, who she is, and why you want her as part of your life. When you begin to be comfortable doing this, try some of the Journeys to visit with her and meet her. Then, when you have a relationship, feel free to begin using the rituals or crafting your own. If you do not have experience with trance journeying, that is okay. I know I was terrible at trance work when I first started down this path. My relationship with Skadi was built on offerings and my attempts to embrace her and her nature through bettering myself. Do what works for you. The important take away isn't how you build the relationship, just that you DO build it before asking for her aid.

Poetry and Prayers

This first section includes poems and prayers to Skadi. I am pleased to say that while I wrote some of them, some of them were shared with me by other members of The Troth and are included here with attribution and permission.

Skalds were prized members of society. They had skills with words that were seen as gifts from the gods, Odin in particular. Writing poetry is hard. Writing good poetry is harder. It is also subjective. Writing poetry in the Norse style of rhyme and rhythm is hardest of all in my humble opinion, which is why I don't attempt it personally. But if you find yourself called to word-art, then by all means write poetry and prayers to the gods. Share them as gifts around their Halls, and honor their names!

"Invocation of Skadi," by Snow

Great Huntress of the North
Lady of the Mountain Paths
Snow Queen
Daughter of Thjazi
Hear us as we call to you!

Snowdis!
As you travel the forest
Hunting with your pack
Help us in our own chases.
Drive the quarry to us,
That we too can sustain our homes.

Skidis!
Fast traveler of the mountain slopes,
Help us avoid the inevitable ruts
That we may move forward
Help us avoid the dangerous ice
That would make us slip and fall.

Daughter of Thjazi,
Share with us
Your inner strength
Your will to address a wrong
To face our fears
No matter the cost or personal price.

Lady of Thrymheim
Let us join your hunt
A member of your pack
A friend around the fire
And in your Hall.

Skadi, Skidis
Be welcome at our fire
Join us at this rite

> Accept our offering of friendship, meat, and drink,
> A gift for a gift.

"Morning Prayer," by Snow

> Hail Skadi!
> Mountain Queen!
> Bright Bride of Gods!
> Grant me your courage
> That I may face my day
> And your strength
> To overcome my trials.

"Prayer Over a Meal," by Snow

> Hail Skadi!
> Huntress and Provider
> Join me at my table
> Share in my bounty
> A Gift for a Gift
> That I may be welcome in your hall!

"Evening Prayer," by Snow

> Máni rises
> I ask your blessing on my rest
> That I may rise with Sunna
> And face the day refreshed
> Ready to meet the challenges it brings
> Hail Skadi!

"In Honour of Skaði," by Timothy "Bjorn" Jones

> Daughter of Storms, you are heir to the great shape-shifter.
> Shadow of Retribution, you feared not the gods, but met them in war-gear.
> Honoured Jötunn, you are respected by the Áss and the Van.
> Companion of Wolves, you chose the solitude of the mountains.

Independent Devourer, you rely on none but yourself.
Slow to Laugh, you are known as wise by the gods.
Spouse of the Sea, nine-nights you longed for the mountains.
Öndurdís, the white-plains and the rocks are your joy.

Inheritor of Thrymheimr, your comfort is the wolf-song.
Binder of Loki, you are long to remember those who slight you.
Visitor of Nóatún, you are the seeker of compromise.
Ski-dís, yours is the hunt of wild beasts.

Watched by the Stars, you are kith to the night sky.
Bringer of Venom, you deliver retribution and revenge.
Bearer to Odin, you are the shining bride of the gods.
Snow Huntress, your skill with the bow always provides.

Skaði, great goddess, your realm is that of Winter.
You are the continuity of cycle, the inevitable change.
You are the consequence to action, bringing timeless justice.
You are the symbol of independence, respected by all.

Hail Skaði! May my life honour you!

"Skaði's Arming," by Ann Gróa Sheffield (copyrighted)

She sees herself take up her spear,
Bow and arrow, armor, helm.
Need and duty drive her on
To do what must be done.

Her weary sadness, doubt and weakness
Shelter in an icy cave
Of frozen tears no flame can touch
Until the task is done.

She sees herself take up her strength:
It rises from the mountain's root,
It rides on wings of winter storm –
In cold and steel she comes.

"For Skadi," by Jennifer Lawrence

>Skadi the fierce, Skadi mountain-tall,
>Skadi winter's huntress:
>the seaside did not suit you,
>all skirling cries of ocean birds
>and the crashing of waves,
>and so you left lovely-footed Njord behind
>and returned to the snow-silent mountains,
>crossing over peak and valley in snowshoes,
>bow in hand, tracking down your hunter's prey.
>The wooded slopes do suit you,
>dark boughs overhead shutting out
>day's brightness, as you seek out
>bear and stag and elk and fox.
>Your weapons are your companions,
>the fine mantle you wear is the arms
>that drape warm around your shoulders,
>and you can go for weeks without speaking,
>needing no idle prattle to be complete.
>Solitude does not trouble you,
>not for you the harshness of bright fires
>and loud voices raised in laughter,
>drunken revelry and the jar and clamor
>of the contest of battle.
>Better, always, the hush of snow on tree boughs,
>and the chill wind between the pines,
>and the eternal allure of following your prey
>through the winter night.

"Encounter in the Snow," by Carl Bonebright

Crying does you no good. Tears freeze, strength warms.

Erik sniffed as the cold air seared his nose, making his eyes water. Father's words had kept tears from spilling down his reddened cheeks for most of the day, but daylight was fading and his failure was near. The wood was quiet and still around him. A thin layer of snow covered the ground, having snuck past the thick branches overhead. His eyes searched the snow for any sign of game, but it was unblemished save for his own rambling tracks. For the tiniest of moments, he allowed himself to give in to despair, to stop trying to swallow the knot in his throat. His family was hungry. They were counting on him.

He would return home again tonight with nothing to show for his work. Father would lie in the corner, his leg propped up, taking far too long to heal. Mother would look up, hope lighting her eyes, only to dull to disappointment before she would smile that hollow we'll-make-it-work-somehow-smile. His sister and brother would be playing on the floor, unaware that tonight they would again get most of the dwindling food. Erik knew he would stare jealously at their plates, knowing it was his own fault and hating himself for hating them.

He cleared his throat loudly and swallowed hard. "No," he said aloud, startling a finch above him. "Not tonight. Tears freeze, strength warms." Eyeing the sun through the trees, he judged he had nearly an hour left before nightfall. Perhaps he could catch a hare. Saliva flooded into his mouth at the thought of hot, roasted game. Erik shook his head and ignored the rumble from his stomach. His numbed fingers tightened on Father's bow as he set off in a new direction, even further from home. He checked the arrows on his hip, making sure they weren't frozen together again. That had cost him a doe last week, but he had told no one how close he had come to such a bounty. Satisfied he wouldn't have to fumble loudly for an arrow, he set off again. Erik pulled his coat a little tighter, feeling the wind caress him as it tried to steal his warmth like a pickpocket from town.

A disturbance in the snow stopped him. The tracks were uneven, and one of the hind legs was barely leaving a mark. He grinned in the fading light. A buck would be nearly impossible to drag back to his home alone, but by the Gods he was going to try! He reached into his quiver and pulled out an arrow, and kissed the tip. He had no idea if that did anything, but it always seemed to work for Father, and tonight he was going to need all the luck he could get. Readying the arrow, Erik made his way through the woods, following the tracks as fast as he dared in the fading light.

Suddenly the buck was before him, hiding at the edge of a clearing. Its neck outstretched and ears perked, the animal was obviously desperate for the greens which still poked through the snow far from the protection of the trees. Erik froze, terrified for a moment that he was upwind and the deer could smell him. A strong breeze snapped through the woods and into his face, which split into a wide grin. He was downwind. Everything was going well, and the buck began to venture into the clearing. The buck's leg appeared broken. It was fortunate Erik managed to cross its track before another predator did. He slid towards the clearing's edge when the sound of a breaking branch shattered the silence of the clearing.

The buck's head shot up from the greens, and Erik despaired. Except the prey wasn't looking his way, its attention was focused on the far side of the clearing. Erik took that opportunity to slip closer, quietly praying that the sound was not someone else after his prey.

The buck went back to the greens, which were already half gone. You're hungry too, huh? thought Erik with a twinge of sympathy. As he began to draw the bow, a flash of movement caught his eye. It was a woman, but not like any woman he had ever seen before. She moved gracefully as a cat, the strength of her limbs singing with every movement. Dressed in white hides, she circled the clearing towards him. Her dark hair fell across her back in a midnight curtain. Her face was a clash of beauty and power.

His shock at the sight of this beautiful woman in what he thought were deserted woods held his jaw open and his tongue still until she was face to face with him. For the briefest of moments, he wondered if she was going to kiss him. As their breaths merged in the air between them, the deer forgotten, a warmth flooded through the young man. He began to speak, but quickly as thought her hand clamped over his mouth and amusement lifted her lips. Her dark eyes looked into his, then to the right. He followed her gaze, belatedly remembered the buck and nodded. Her hand moved from his mouth and gestured for him to draw the bow.

Confused, he shrugged and notched the arrow again, drawing the bow as his father had taught him, and prepared to loose the arrow. He nearly let go in shock when he felt her hands on his arms, lifting his elbow and straightening his shoulders. He shot a glance at the woman, but she pointed back to the buck. Returning his attention to the deer, he noticed the greens were almost gone. Time was running out once more. His arms began to strain from holding the arrow at the ready for so long, his muscles unused to the heavier draw of his father's bow. He sighted the arrow and prepared to fire.

"Wait..." a voice whispered in his ear. Somehow the woman was behind him and held his hands so delicately, he was not even sure she was touching him. A pressure so slight it might have been an errant breeze adjusted his aim up and to the left. "Now."

The bowstring slipped from his fingertips with a whisper, and the KWANG of it returning to rest surprised him so much that he jumped, falling on his butt. He looked about, but the mysterious woman was gone. He looked around and saw the tracks of her approach, but no evidence of her departure. Then it occurred to him he hadn't heard the buck cry out. Disappointment flooded him as he realized he must have missed completely, the injured animal running off while he was sitting stupidly in the snow. Turning, he saw a heavy, dark shape in the center of the clearing, unmoving. Disbelief etched onto his face, he edged out towards the buck, quickly notching another arrow just in case the buck leaped up again. Finally he was close enough to see that his shot had been perfect. Right through the eye, the buck had been dead before it hit the ground. He removed the arrow from the carcass and looked around again for the mysterious woman, to no avail.

Two hours later he finally made it home. The light shown from the windows flickered as he watched Mother's shadow pace, watching for his return. He was late, but he knew there would be celebration this evening, full bellies all around, and a strange tale to tell.

He smiled, filled with pure happiness for the first time in a long while. He would look around with pride at the table tonight. His sister and brother would sleep well, and no one would resent a little extra left on their plates, aware of how big brother had brought food home for everyone. Mother's eyes would light up at the sight of a healthy catch, and tears of joy would spot her cheeks as she helped clean the carcass. Father would smile with pride and relief.

Some day, Erik would sit at his own table in the early winter darkness, sharing a meal with a wife and children. He would tell his wide-eyed sons why hunting arrows are kissed before the kill, and the tale of the Lady who helped him hunt when he needed it most.

"When Wolves Howl," by Diana L. Paxson

> When wolves howl upon the mountain heights,
> Swift, beneath the northern lights,
> Skadhi comes skimming o'er the snow,
> When it goes,
> Her sweet buds will swell the bough,
> Earth will open to the plough.

When Wolves Howl

words: Diana L. Paxson
tune: traditional Norse

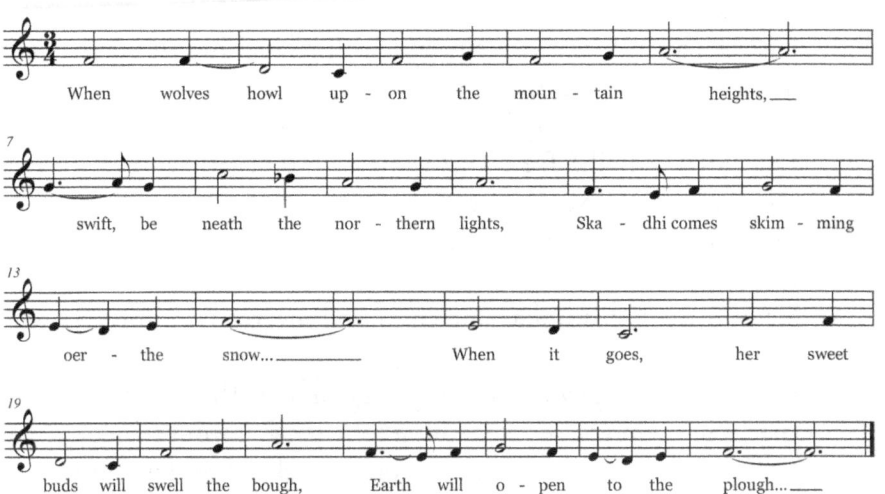

When wolves howl up-on the moun-tain heights,
swift, be-neath the nor-thern lights, Ska-dhi comes skim-ming
oer the snow... When it goes, her sweet
buds will swell the bough, Earth will o-pen to the plough...

Journeys

If you are new to Journey-work and trance, I would highly recommend Diana Paxson's book *Trance-portation* as a primer to get you started. Basic techniques such as grounding and centering, concentration exercises, and other such skills are critical for success in this arena. To that end, I am writing this section for those who already have the basics of this sort of work. If you don't, then there are many authors and teachers better qualified than I to get you on the right path.

If, however, you do have the basics down, then one of the best ways to connect with Skadi, and indeed many beings, is through trance: journeying to meet them on their home turf, as it were. Our gods take their hospitality seriously, though, so if you wish to visit Thrymheim, make sure to take a gift for Skadi with you.

For all of these scripts, I assume you have a way of getting to the Yggdrasil already, and using the Tree to travel between the realms, or some other "home base" that allows you to move between the realms. If not, again, I would recommend *Trance-portation*, as setting up this part of trance work is a fundamental skill that is built on in Diana Paxson's book.

Also, and I feel this is critical, please keep the following in mind as you work with spirit allies or trance in general:

1. Do not demand the spirit's name. Instead, ask what it would like to be called.
2. Heathenry, and indeed pretty much all related Indo-European traditions, are based on the concept of "a gift for a gift." If you wish to make a friend or strengthen a friendship, take a gift.
3. DO NOT ACCEPT FOOD while in the other realms from random spirits. Or even non-random spirits. Take food with you and remember Persephone's fate and that of many who get trapped by the Fair Folk.
4. Stay on the paths unless and until you are very comfortable with spirit work.
5. Have a plan for how you're going to get home. That can be someone checking in on you, or something to recall you from trance such as is usually incorporated into drumming tracks (three loud hits at the end).

A Visit to Thrymheim

The following is a script to get to Thrymheim and meet Skadi. It is a script that works for me and how I envision the path there. As always, your mileage may vary. Some people like very specific trance inductions, and some don't. I made this one fairly specific, as I find it's easier to remove detail from directions than add it if you haven't been somewhere before.

Close your eyes and take a deep breath. And another. Breath in. . . and out. . . . In. . . and out. . .

As you breathe, feel the air around you begin to cool. The temperature drops, slowly at first, then more quickly. There is a bite in the air and a cold breeze blows, shaking the pine trees so that they whisper to you and making your breath come out in clouds.

Looking around you, there is a shimmering landscape covered in snow. The tree branches sparkle like they are covered in diamonds and the sky is a bright blue. The sun shines overhead, and there are no clouds to hide the mountain peaks that rise around you, climbing over the canopy of tree limbs on either side of the path that winds over little bumps and dips in the snow. Upon the path are two tracks, clearly made by skis.

Follow the tracks up the side of the mountain as the path begins to climb. The trees begin to thin and be replaced by rocky outcroppings, then hard granite blocks glittering in the bright sunlight with ice and quartz crystals.

The path widens, more regularly travelled, and the ski tracks are joined by the impression of snowshoes and animals. In the snow you see signs of wolf, deer, fox, bear, and rabbit… and some you don't recognize. The land here is wild and untamed.

The path rises above the tree line. Without the trees to break the wind, you watch as it picks up the dry snow, swirling it around in the air. A particularly harsh gust makes it impossible to see for a moment, but as the snow settles once more, you catch your first glimpse of it: Thrymheim. The Noisy Hall. Built of the same granite that forms the mountains, it too sparkles in the sunlight. A thin crust of ice catches the light and dazzles the eye as you make your way up the now steep path to the massive iron oak gates, carved with fanciful images of beasts cavorting in the snow.

You knock, and the gates open, admitting you to a courtyard where a large beast is spitted over a fire and a cauldron bubbles with something that smells amazing, the scent carrying easily on the cold mountain air.

On the other side of the courtyard is the entrance to the Keep and standing just outside the open doors is a woman wearing hunting leathers and a thick fur cloak of some white beast. She smiles at you, her eyes twinkling with good humor. Approach her and meet Skadi.

Journey to the Cave

While, in my experience, the gods are happy to have us visit their halls and to offer us hospitality when we do so, it isn't necessarily where the real work occurs. My work with Skadi tends to occur in one of two places: out in the woods, or in the Cave. The cave is where I met my first spirit guide, where I learned to take on other forms in my journeys, and where I do much of my training. Some people call it an Inner Hall. For me, though, this is more like an inner hall where I do my trance work with Skadi and the rest of Her Pack, rather than my own personal refuge.

You stand at a fork in the path, the snow swirling around you. One direction curls up the side of the mountain towards the peak, where you can just make out the flickering torches at the gate to Thrymheim.

But today, you take the other path. In this direction the path leads to the base of the mountain. As you reach what seems like a dead end, you find a boulder that has dislodged itself from above and tumbled down the mountain, almost concealing the entrance to a cave. You can smell the smoke of fire that permeates the air as if it has been burning since time immemorial, scented with the resin of pine and fir and incense. The mouth of the cave is covered by a thick leather baffle to keep out the wind.

Push it aside and enter the cave. Look around.

In the middle of the chamber is a fire, surrounded by piles of furs and leather pads. At the rear of the cave is a small stream, the water clear. There is a sense of purpose in the air, of expectation, as if someone has been waiting for you. If you brought an offering, make it to the fire. Otherwise, choose a place to settle in and wait. It won't be long now. . . .

Finding Your Fylgja

This part of the trance picks up in the Cave where we left off. As I said, many of the trance inductions I use with Skadi happen in or leave from the Cave.

A *fylgja* is one of the parts of the soul in Germanic tradition. The word means "to accompany" and the concept is similar to that of the Irish Fetch. The word can also refer to the afterbirth. Typically, the fylgja takes an animal form, and some say that what kind of animal is shown by what creature comes to eat the afterbirth, usually carrion eaters including such animals as mice, dogs, cats, foxes, and crows (Turville-Petre, "Dreams in Icelandic Tradition," pp. 93-111). Another view of fylgja is that they take the form of an animal that represents the innate characteristics of the person they are connected to, not unlike the idea of a spirit animal in other traditions (Jennbert, "The Heroized Dead," p. 137).

If you already work with spirit allies, then use this trance as an opportunity to deepen that relationship. If not, then use it as a chance to forge some new alliances.

Journey to the cave and make yourself comfortable. As you settle on a cushion, remove your pack from your back. Open the pack and find food and drink, and as you relax in the warmth of the flickering flame, pour yourself a drink.

As the logs crackle, you close your eyes and reach deep into yourself. In this place, you can feel the various parts of yourself. The part that feels a childlike wonder for the world around you. The part that analyzes every situation for a hidden threat. And there, glancing at you from the shadows, the part of you that shows your true nature. It is hidden, looking through your eyes so that you cannot yet see it, but you can feel it.

Call it forth with an offering. Show it your hand as friend. Be patient, for it has been hidden for a long time. Give it a gift, then settle in to wait. Like a wild animal, it may take time and patience for it to show itself to you, but if you speak softly and make no sudden movements, it will.

You can use a similar process to find other allies.

When you arrive at the cave this time, make sure to ward it against anything that means you ill. Settle in as before, but this time instead of turning your attention inside, you will be turning it outside. Think about the sort of aid that you need from this alliance. What are you willing to offer, what do you wish to get?

Perhaps you need a swift ally to fly with you? Or an ally that will guard your back? Maybe you need an ally who has many friends and can introduce you to others, or maybe you need an ally who can teach you to hunt? Whatever it is you seek, make sure that it is crystal clear in your mind. Also make sure that you know what you are willing to barter in return. Remember, a gift for a gift. The more specific the better. Don't make open ended promises here!

Once you have those conditions firmly in your mind, whisper them onto the wind. Send your thought out into the otherworlds, then wait here, in the Cave, behind your wards. It may take some time, so feel free to enjoy the food and drink you brought with you.

When something responds, welcome it into the cave under the condition that it comes in peace and means you no harm. If it comes inside, offer it a drink, either of what you brought or from the spring at the back of the cave and ask it what it wishes to be called. Graciously use the name it gives you and ask it what it is willing to barter with you. Remember, you can make counter offers, and don't promise anything you either can't deliver or don't feel comfortable about.

If you strike a bargain, invite it to join you at the fire, or to walk the paths of Thrymheim with it, so that you can get to know each other. Make your exchanges in good faith, but also with wariness, and don't let it lead you off the path on this first encounter unless you are already very comfortable in this realm. When you are ready to depart, be clear with when you will return and what you will be bringing, and also what you expect of your new friend. Clear communication is key!

Rites

When it comes to rituals, everyone has their own favorite way to do things. But whether the ritual is Druidic, Wiccan, Heathen, or Catholic, there are a few parts to the ritual structure that all good rituals incorporate. Most of the successful rituals I have experienced incorporate a five-stage structure that delineates a dramatic flow of energy. These five stages might be likened to acts of Shakespeare's plays. The flow of dramatic energy is introduced, built upon, reaches its crescendo, begins to dissipate, and then terminates in a satisfactory manner (Ray, "The Five-Act Play"). It has been said this five act dramatic structure lends itself well to religious ritual, and historically has operated within the Indo-European religious framework (Bonewits, *Neopagan Rites*, pp. 23-24). This is the framework that my family hearth, Kindred, and more and more the public rituals we participate in use.

Framework:

I. Introduction. The altar or ritual ground is prepared and purified. The participants assemble and are ritually purified. The presiding officiant welcomes the participants and formally states the purpose of said ritual.

II. Rising Action. The deities or spirits are invoked according to whatever mechanisms the spiritual traditions dictate.

III. Climax. Offerings are made to the deities or spirits in whatever proscribed manner. Usually the presiding officiant consecrates the offerings with a formal prayer.

IV. Falling Action. With the deities or spirits invited and placated, the participants can perform various workings in their name. These can be esoteric workings, readings from the relevant lore, or a communal activity.

V. Conclusion. The deities or spirits are thanked for their participation. There are closing prayers, and the participants are dismissed.

As you can see, these various elements can be adapted to your personal practice. Some groups purify with a circle, with incense, or with a hammer rite. The specifics are not important and should reflect your group or personal preferences. The important part is how you make the energy flow between parts of the ritual.

A Ritual to Skadi for Aid in Lean Times

Items: Food and Drink, offering bowl, your purification preference, your tool for taking an omen, an item to hold her blessing (I use a quartz crystal or a piece of blue cyanite, but anything that makes you think of Her would work). For the drink, make sure you have enough to share with yourself, and that it is something you are willing to drink or eat, too.

Purpose: The purpose of this ritual is to ask for Skadi to bless you and see you through the lean times. Skadi is a huntress and feels a keen responsibility for her kin that they have the sustenance that they need. Though we are no longer a society where the majority of us hunt and farm to provide our food, many of us still face lean times and live paycheck to paycheck.

Introduction: Purify your area in whatever way you prefer. I personally like to light incense (pine or juniper or fir for Skadi) and smudge the area down. Personal purification is also a preference. For a solo ritual, I take a shower before beginning. In a group setting, you could sprinkle people with water or use the incense on them as well.

Rising Action: For this ritual, I invoke not only Skadi, but the Ancestors as well. Some I call by name, some I call in a general invitation to ancestors. This is important because while not everyone is on good terms with their immediate ancestors and family, it is important to remember that you are the product of hundreds of ancestors, many of whom sacrificed and survived the lean times that you would be here today. If you're calling specific ancestors, especially those who you knew in life, then I would also include a beverage or snack they were particularly fond of. In my family, that's coffee or bourbon. Overall, I find that a cup of coffee or tea is usually a happy offering for my ancestors, especially if I'm in financial hardships.

For Skadi, I like to make offerings to her and her Pack. If I have it, then vodka is (in my experience) her favorite beverage, especially if I keep it in the freezer. I also try, if I can, to make an offering of raw meat for the Pack. If not, then any snack I have on hand that my own dog would eat is usually accepted. Again, lean times means that the Pack understands hardship.

Also note that usually main offerings come in the next phase, but in a solo ritual, I like to make them as I invoke the beings, much like I offer a cup of coffee or tea to guests when they enter my home.) And so you will see offerings made in this section.

The words you use are better if they come from your heart, but if you are struggling to find words, here is an example of what I say. I call on the bloodline first, then close known ancestors, then Skadi.

> Ancestors, both ancient and near!
> Hear me now as I call to you!
> You who gave of your blood, sweat, and tears!
> You who died that your line might live!
> Hear me now as I call to you!
> *(pour offering to ancestors)*

> Grandma!
> You who taught me to cook
> And stayed up with me at night when I was sick.
> You who kept our family together and helped us when we struggled,
> I call out to you!
> *(pour offering to Grandma)*

> Papa! You who worked long hours to provide for us!
> You who taught me to build and drive!
> I call out to you!
> *(pour offering for Grandpa)*

> Skadi! Lady of the Mountain Fastness!
> Goddess of the Hunt!
> Bring your Pack and Join me in this right!
> Snowdis, I call out to you!
> *(make offering for Skadi and the Pack)*

Climax: Now that Skadi and the Ancestors are present, it is time to share with them your struggles, telling them what you need and asking their wisdom and blessings on your endeavors. This is, of course, intensely personal and will vary based on what it is you really do need. A job? A better job? A roommate to split the bills? Don't be afraid to ask for aid, but also know that Skadi is only going to give it to you if you've done your due diligence in pursuing it already. That said, She understands how hard it can be to overcome inertia (speaking from experience here!) so if that is what is holding you back, admit it, and ask her to help you get off your behind! Of course, be prepared to follow through!

> (*Pour a cup of coffee, tea, vodka, or whatever you are using for yourself and take a sip, then pour a sip's worth into your offering bowl*)

Thank you for joining me today. Thank you for hearing me and making the journey. Be welcome in my [*space/home/circle/etc.*]

(*Take another sip and pour*)

I find myself in the Lean Times. I am [*between paychecks/out of work/etc.*] and need Your Help. The cupboards are bare and my bank account is empty and I'm not sure where to go from here.

(*Take another sip and pour*)

Lady, you Hunt on behalf of the Folk and keep them from starvation. I ask that you and your Pack bless my hunt, or join me in it, that I too may find success.

(*Take another sip and pour*)

Falling Action: In this section, we begin to internalize the energy that so far has been outside of us. The first step will be to take an omen by whatever your preferred method. Personally, I use Runes, but Ogham, Tarot, or other Oracles work just as well. I do find, though, in working with Skadi, that she is clearest in Runes.

Lady, what actions would you have me take? What message do you have to give?

(*Take omen*)

Spend some time meditating on the omen. What are the different meanings or interpretations of it? If you did a pull of more than one rune or card, how do they relate to each other? When you feel you understand the message, then you will imbue that energy into the object you brought for this purpose. For example, if the message is that you need to cultivate stamina (I get this one a lot!) then I might galdor (chant) a *sowilo* rune into the object. If I need to break out of a pattern, it might be *nauthiz*. Pour the energy into the object until you feel as if it can't hold any more, then dip the object into the offering bowl to seal the energy.

Conclusion: Thank everyone for joining you. Let them know you appreciate them, that you are grateful for their aid and energy in the working and that you will continue to call on them outside of ritual.

> Lady of Thrymheim,
> Wild Huntress,
> Thank you for aiding me today!
> Your counsel is as wise as your feet are sure,
> And I am grateful for your gifts.
> See me through this lean time,
> And join me again in a time of plenty!
> Hail Skadi!
> (*pour out a small offering*)
>
> Ancestors, you who lived in times past,
> Who survived the lean times that I might be born!
> Thank you for your aid,
> Your descendent remembers you!
> Hail the Ancestors!
> (*pour out the last of the offering*)

If you have candles or incense lit, blow them out, or wait for them to go out while thinking about the messages you received and making plans for how to overcome your obstacles. Then ACTUALLY DO IT!

A Ritual to Skadi for Blessing Your Tools

This is a short ritual I use when I acquire a new ritual tool. It's simple, and I don't bother with many of the steps outlined in the ritual for Lean Times. The point of this ritual is to consecrate the tool. I use a variation of this ritual for any tool that is being dedicated to a specific being. For example, my Thor's Hammer used a variation where I called on Him. The items I have dedicated to Skadi are a hunting knife, a horn, an axe, and a set of runes.

Items: Offering (I use vodka), offering bowl, incense (I use pine), something to sprinkle vodka with (like a sprig from a pine tree), and item being consecrated.

I like to lay my tools out on the altar ahead of time. My altar for Skadi has a statue of her, an offering bowl, previously consecrated tools as listed above, a horn and candle.

Fill the horn with vodka (or other liquid offering) and light the incense and candle if you are using one. Purify yourself and your space however you usually do (see Ritual for Lean Times for purification ideas). For a short ritual like this, I smudge the space, the altar, and myself with the incense, then inhale deeply, letting the pine scent remind me of the wild places Skadi prefers (I live in a city).

> Lady, you who haunt the wilderness, bringing home the fruits of your labors
> Hear me now as I call to you!
> Snowdis, You who rely on your tools to feed the folk and defend the realm,
> I have acquired a new tool for Our Work!
> Skadi, Snowdis, join me at my altar and bless this tool that it may serve us well!
> Hail Skadi!
> *(Pour a drink of vodka from the horn into the bowl)*

Pick up the tool and hold it over the altar, pass it through the incense smoke, and spend some time meditating on the tool and how you will use it in your work. For example, is it a drum to aid you in your journeying? A knife to cut spiritual bindings? A bow and arrow for archery practice to bring you closer to Her? Imagine using the item with her aid. How will it serve both of your purposes?

Once you have the answer to these questions firmly in mind, ask her to imbue the tool with her power. Concentrate on how you will use the tool while holding it with your eyes closed and say something along the lines of,

> This hunting horn will be used to call the Folk to Ritual that we may reaffirm and build our community. Snowdis, as one who provides for your Kin, bless this Horn with your gift that when we summon the folk with it, they find their way through our modern wilderness to the community they seek!

Or maybe:

> Skadi, while there are some bindings we choose, there are others that are unhealthy for us. Bless this knife that when we are faced with a painful, frightening task, we may find the bravery you did in marching on Asgard to cut ourselves free!

Once you have invoked her over the tool, pour a drink of vodka from the horn into the bowl, then dip the sprig or twig into the bowl and use it to sprinkle vodka on the tool. One of the reasons I like vodka for this is it doesn't dry sticky, so if you choose something else you might want to keep that in mind.

As you asperge the item, feel Skadi's blessing flow from the bowl into it. Close with your gratitude.

> Skadi, Huntress and Lady of Thrymheim,
> Thank you for your aid in this.
> May your sword be ever sharp, and your quiver ever full.
> May this [*name of object*] serve Your purpose in my hand,
> Hail Huntress!

Ritual to End a Relationship

Perhaps one of the aspects of Skadi's story that is most unique is the fact that she divorces Njord. There doesn't seem to be any animosity in their divorce, merely that things weren't working out. Their desires for the future were incompatible: he wanted the beaches and she wanted the mountains. There is a lesson here for modern times. So often, people stay in loveless marriages or incompatible relationships out of fear: fear of the unknown, fear of being or dying alone, fear of not being able to make it on their own.

As a modern society, we spend a lot of time planning the rituals to join people together, but we have very few rituals to end a relationship. I know when I got divorced, we spent maybe ninety seconds in front of the judge and then it was over. Sixteen years of marriage, just done and over.

Now, I was lucky in that we managed our divorce without too much acrimony and blame. We both wanted out, we didn't have much in the way of worldly goods, and we didn't have kids. As divorces go, it was easy enough. But it still wasn't easy.

This ritual is designed to be done alone, but I will also offer suggestions on how to alter it if you and the other person in the relationship are on speaking terms enough to end the relationship ritually together. If so, it is much more potent. Also, if you made oaths to each other in front of witnesses, having one of those witnesses present to release your oaths is also very powerful.

You will need incense for smudging, something that represents your relationship such as binding cords or a photo of the two (or more) of you or the unity candle from your wedding, and something sharp to cut that object with. If it is something burnable, and you have a safe way of burning it without setting off fire alarms, then burning works too. Or both. Depends on how much closure you need.

Begin by purifying the location and yourself in whatever way you prefer. I would recommend you cleanse with mugwort.

If there were people at the original binding ceremony who can be present and whom you would want present, then invite them and thank them for attending. This is particularly good if you were formally wed. Remember, a wedding is a public oath taking, and when the officiant asks if there is anyone there with reason you shouldn't be wed, that's the modern equivalent of the community holding your oath as they would in sumble. Thus, having a representative there who held your oath is a good idea, but this may not be feasible.

Invite the ancestors to witness. They, after all, have a very strong desire to see you happy, and to see their descendants prosper. Even if you are not close to the last few generations of your blood family, you can invite the ancestors who support you, the ancestors of blood, and of spirit, and heart and community who strove to allow you the freedom to choose your own partners, and end relationships on your terms. Because no matter how formal the relationship, or what sexual orientation or gender identity the participants, the right and ability to choose to enter into relationships (romantic or not) is a relatively modern one that had to be fought for.

> Ancestors of blood and bone,
> You who struggled to subsist in hard times
> You who fought for the chance to be true to yourselves!
> Join me at this rite, as I once more choose my own path.
> Walk with me, that I do not walk alone.

Njord yearning for the sea.
Envisioned by W. G. Collingwood, in Bray, *The Elder or Poetic Edda* (1908)

Next invite Skadi. A possible invocation is:

> Skadi!
> Huntress of the North!
> You who refuse to be confined to a path chosen by others, but instead seek your own fulfillment!
> Join me today as I sever these cords that bind me into a role that no longer fits.
> Help me to be Hale and Whole as I continue my path!
> Skadi, join us at this rite!

If the person you were sharing an oathbond with is there, then ask each other to be released. You might try something like:

> No one can predict how we will grow in life
> And life without growth is no life.
> An oath made with the best of intentions can no longer be kept
> And so now, I ask you, will you release me of this bond
> That we may find our own truths
> And walk our own paths
> In Frith for what was?

Skadi yearning for the mountains.
Envisioned by W. G. Collingwood, in Bray, *The Elder or Poetic Edda* (1908)

If there are people there who were also at your original ritual/wedding, then ask them to release you of your oath as well.

> Witnesses who bore our oath
> Who gave it weight in the Well
> Unweave with me the Wyrd
> That we may once more walk alone?

Next, take the object that represents your relationship. Hold it in your hands and think about all that the relationship was to you. Think about the good times that made you happy and the bad times that made you cry. Allow yourself grief. Acknowledge your feelings, whether they are relief or failure or anything and everything else. It is all valid. Don't rush through this part. Think about why you sought the relationship in the first place, and when you knew that it wasn't working. Cry if it feels right. Or scream. Channel all those thoughts and feelings into the object that you're holding until you can truly let it all go.

When you feel as if you have emptied as much of yourself into the object as you can, then either cut the object or burn it. Personally, I prefer burning. I find it cathartic, but it may not be practical for your living situation.

When the object is destroyed, either cut into tiny pieces or burned to ash, then make the remains an offering to Skadi.

> Skadi, you who found your power within yourself,
> Accept this offering.
> It represents my new beginning
> As I reclaim myself.
> Aid me as I move past this pain
> And start my life anew.
> Help me find my purpose
> That I may be my best self.
> Skadi, bless me now and always.
> Hail Skadi!

Now, thank the beings who attended for their support. If you had friends or family with you, thank each of them individually for the roles they've played in getting you through this. If they are there with you, this would be a good time for them to share with you something positive about you, some way they have seen your strength or seen you grow.

Thank the ancestors for blessing you and attending the ritual, then make sure that any fire is extinguished and share a last drink.

Obviously, there are other ways that this ritual can be used. Ending relationships isn't the only time we need to cut something toxic out of our lives. It is an obvious one, though, because it is a time when others witness our oaths.

Other times we might need a ritual like this is when we leave a toxic job or quit school. Any time you are trying to reinvent yourself, then a ritual along these lines would be appropriate.

Joining the Pack

This section is a ritual to join Skadi's hunting pack. As a member of the pack, you take on the role of hunting that which would harm the folk, of providing for the folk, and Her hunting magic. Joining the pack is not something to undertake lightly: it is a real commitment. Until and unless you are prepared to keep it, I wouldn't recommend making this pledge. I wouldn't recommend doing it until you are very comfortable working with

Her energy, and truly feel called to this path. That said, for those of us who do feel Her Call, joining the pack gives you a sense of belonging and allies in her wild realm.

To begin with, purify yourself and your space in whatever way you normally begin rituals. I usually take a bath with a combination of Epsom salt and fresh peppermint (which I have an abundance of in my garden). To clear the area, I usually use some variation of pine, mugwort, or balsam incense.

Some heathens like to wear ritual garb or have specific things they wear for trance and ritual work. Personally, I have a pendent that I wear when I am working with Skadi that is in the form of a chain mail snowflake. To me, this represents both her comfort in winter and in garments of war. If you have ceremonial regalia, then by all means use it. The purpose of such is to put oneself in the mindset that this is a special, magical, esoteric, religious time and separate from the mundane, after all.

Once I and the space feel right, I light the candles on Her altar and make offerings to Her and to her Wolves. Since I tend to do my work with her at night, I save a plate of whatever I had for dinner for her and the Wolves, and put that along with a strong shot of vodka on her altar, inviting them to partake of what I provided for my family. If I don't have something for dinner that feels appropriate, then I make an offering of fresh raw meat to the Wolves (I find they like offal and raw bones a lot). Usually though, our family meal is some variation of meat and vegetables, and they seem fine with a slice of our pork roast. Given that this is a special occasion, though, you might want to go all out and get them the raw meat, regardless of what you had yourself.

What you choose to take your oath on is up to you. Some heathens use an oath ring for such occasions. For this, you may choose to use the oath ring, or you may instead swear an oath on something to represent Her Pack. I chose to swear on a hunting knife that I have dedicated to Her.

While holding the object, repeat the following oath:

"I, (your name, magical or mundane), pledge myself to the Pack. I will share with the Pack my knowledge, my skills, and my will. I will choose Honor and Frith. I will defend the Pack in good times and bad to the best of my abilities. When She Calls, I will answer."

Seal the oath with a shared drink. If you make the oath on an object, it is a good idea to blood the object to seal it and the oath, but this isn't required.

Welcome to the Pack! This is a good time to do the Journey to Meet the Pack! I'll look for you in the cave!

Journey to Meet the Pack

This induction should only be done AFTER you choose to Join the Pack. I cannot stress this enough. Do NOT do this if you have not already pledged yourself to the Pack.

For this journey, make your way to the Cave. You should have already made that part of the journey before, at the very least to find it, to meet your fylgja, and to spend some time in Her Wilds. Now it is time to meet the Others in the Pack.

Once you reach the cave, settle in. Find a spot that is comfortable for you. Breath the scent of pine branches burning in the fire. Feel the occasional draft that makes it past the leather baffle at the opening of the cave. Water drips somewhere as an icicle melts in the ambient heat.

Outside over the sounds of the wind comes the creak of footsteps in snow. A gloved hand pushes back the baffle and a large figure steps inside. On either side of the figure follow a canine. At first, you assume wolves, but it's hard to tell. Whatever they are, they are large, furry, and in tune with Her.

She pushes back her hood and smiles at you, and the canines come closer, sniffing you and wagging their bushy tails.

"Sit, beasts," a voice rumbles, the sounds of an avalanche hidden within. It's a voice that seems like it should be loud, and yet it is barely above a whisper. The sound travels in the cave, though, and the beasts sit obediently. Her eyes turn to you. "Welcome. Tonight, we hunt."

More people are joining you. Some with dogs, some with wolves, some alone, and some with other creatures, for the Pack has all kinds in it of both people and beast. Once everyone has arrived, Skadi lifts her hunting horn and blows a blast that makes the walls of the cave tremble. Her eyes meet those of everyone present, you last of all, and She smiles.

"The Pack Grows. Meet our new mate. Welcome them. And then, the Mountain waits!" she announces. There is a murmur from the rest of the pack, and then, as quickly as they arrive, they surround you and begin to lead you out into the wilderness.

A full Hunter's Moon shines overhead, the light making the snow look like glitter. Tonight, you avoid the paths. Tonight, you travel with the Pack. The Horn sounds again, and as one, you move out to Hunt.

Conclusions

While there are many holes in what we know about Skadi (and most of the Æsir, Vanir, and their allies) based on the Lore alone, there is enough surviving material about Skadi to weave together an understanding of her character.

This begins with understanding her father. Thjazi was a powerful Jotun, capable of magic and shapeshifting, wealthy in gold and land, and with aspirations to increase his reach. As his only child, Skadi was clearly raised to be a strong and powerful being in her own right. Fiercely independent and willing to face down the might of the Æsir to collect their debt for her father's death, she presents typically masculine social traits to a reader. Yet she shows concern for her step-son and does later have children with Odin, showing at least some maternal side.

While her collection of weregild likely falls within the realms of the law as defined by *Grágas*, it is an unusual circumstance as we are unclear whether her uncles were still alive. Even if they were not, given the vastness of the clan structure outlined in Icelandic Law and the number of Jotuns there should have been other parties responsible for Thjazi's weregild. Based on the implications of *Hyndluljóð*, she should not have been tapped as the party responsible for collecting weregild, for negotiating her own marriage, or for inheriting Thrymheim. And yet, she does not shirk her duty to her kin or her family honor. There is a lesson in this for modern Heathens: sometimes we must break social norms and expectations to be true to ourselves and our kin.

Skadi is strong and fierce. She is at home in the wild and thrives in places that would kill a weaker being. In fact, her chosen home is called Noisy Hall. Her favorite music is the wind in the trees and the howling of wolves. Strong in more than body and mind, she has magic that she inherited from her father and that the Allfather sought for his sons.

While she demands much of us, she gives much in return. While she pushes us, she is not cruel and does not seek to see us break. She has no use for the broken, for those who seek an easy path and are unwilling to take responsibility for themselves. Rather, she rewards bravery and self-determination.

She has little interest in your outward characteristics. She doesn't care if you're man, woman, neither, or both. She doesn't care who you choose to take to your bed, so long as bedding happens with consent and honor.

I hope that you found something here of worth, something that expands your knowledge or your practice. Should you have feedback or questions, I can be reached at niedfyre@gmail.com.

Hail the Folk! Hail Skadi!

—Snow

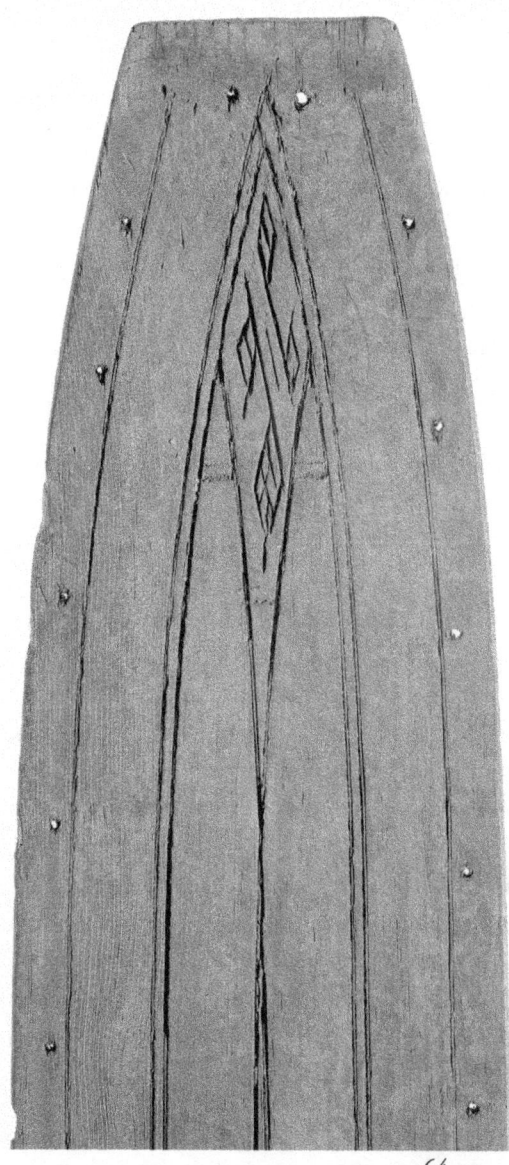

Carved wooden ski from Steinhaugmo, Nordland, Norway, dated to the late Viking Age. The holes along the sides were for attaching leather or fir to the bottom for better traction, like the "climbing skins" still used by backcountry skiers. Photo by P. Fredriksen, NTNU Vitenskapsmuseet, CC BY-SA 4.0.

Works Cited

Bonewits, Isaac. *Neopagan Rites: A Guide to Creating Rituals That Work*. Woodbury: Llewellyn Publications, 2007.

Dennis, Andrew, Peter Foote, and Richard Perkins, ed. *Grágas I: Laws of Early Iceland*. Winnipeg: University of Manitoba Press, 2014.

Dodds, Jeramy (transl.) *The Poetic Edda*. Toronto: Coach House Books, 2014.

Hollander, Lee M (transl.) *The Poetic Edda*. Austin: University of Texas Press, 2008.

Jennbert, Kristina. "The Heroized Dead: People, Animals, and Materiality in Scandinavian Death Rituals, AD 200–1000." Anders Andrén, Kristina Jennbert, and Catharina Raudvere (eds.). *Old Norse Religion in Long-Term Perspectives: Origins, Changes, and Interactions*. Lund: Nordic Academic Press, 2006. pp. 135-140.

Jochens, Jenny. *Women in Old Norse Society*. Ithaca: Cornell University Press, 1995.

Lusch-Schreiwer, Robert. "About Urglaawe." Retrieved from Urglaawe: http://www.urglaawe.net January 7, 2019.

McGrath, Sheena. *Njord and Skadi: A Myth Explored*. London: Avalonia, 2015. E-book.

Miller, William. "Some Aspects of Householding in the Medieval Icelandic Commonwealth." *Continuity and Change*, vol. 3, no. 3 (1988), pp. 321-355.

Poole, Russel. "(Introduction to) Eyvindr skáldaspillir Finnsson, Háleygjatal." Diana Whaley (ed.), *Poetry from the Kings' Sagas 1: From Mythical Times to c. 1035. Skaldic Poetry of the Scandinavian Middle Ages 1*. Brepols, Turnhout, 2012. p. 195. http://skaldic.abdn.ac.uk/db.php?id=1186&if=default&table=text&val=edition

Ray, Rebecca. "The Five Act Play (Dramatic Structure)." n.d. Web. 18 March 2019. <https://www.storyboardthat.com/articles/e/five-act-structure>.

Schröder, Franz Rolf. *Skadi und die Götter Skandinaviens*. Tübingen: J. C. B. Mohr, 1941.

Simek, Rudolf. *Dictionary of Northern Mythology.* Trans. Angela Hall. Cambridge: D.S. Brewer, 1993.

Sturlason, Snorre. *Heimskringla or The Lives of the Norse Kings.* Ed. Erling Monsen. Trans. A. H. Smith. New York: Dover Publications, 1932.

Sturluson, Snorri. *The Prose Edda.* Trans. Jesse Byock. London: Penguin Books, 2005.

Turville-Petre, E.O.G. "Dreams in Icelandic Tradition." *Folklore*, vol. 69, no. 2 (1958), pp 93-111.

Turville-Petre, E.O.G. *Myth and Religion of the North: The Religion of Ancient Scandinavia.* Westport: Greenwood Press, 1964.

Sources of Illustrations

Bray, Olive (W. G. Collingwood, illust.) *The Elder or Poetic Edda, Commonly Known as Saemund's Edda. Part I—The Mythological Poems.* London: The Viking Club, 1908.

Foster, Mary H. and Mabel H. Cummings. *Asgard Stories: Tales from Norse Mythology.* New York: Silver, Burdett and Co., 1901.

Guerber, H. A. *Myths of the Norsemen from the Eddas and Sagas.* London: George C. Harrap, 1919.

Keary, A. and E. (Louis Huard, illust.) *The Heroes of Asgard: Tales from Scandinavian Mythology.* New York: Macmillan & Co., 1909.

Klugh, Maria C. *Tales from the Far North.* Chicago: A. Flanagan, 1909.

Olaus Magnus. *Historia de gentibus septentrionalibus.* Rome, 1555.

Sander, Fredrik. *Edda Sämund den Vises: skaldeverk af fornordiska myt- och hjältesånger om de götiska eller germaniska folkens gamla gudatro, sagominnen och vandringar.* Stockholm: P. A. Norstedt & Söner, 1893.

Scheffer, Johannes Gerhard. *Lapponia: id est, regionis Lapponum et gentis nova et verissima descriptio.* Frankfurt: Christian Wolff, 1673.

Wägner, W., and M. W. MacDowall (W. S. W. Anson, ed.). *Asgard and the Gods: The Tales and Traditions of our Northern Ancestors, Forming a Complete Manual of Norse Mythology.* London: Swan, Sonnenschein, Le Bas and Lowrey, 1886.

About the Author

Rev. Laura "Snow" Fuller joined the Troth and co-founded North Star Kindred (NSK) in the Lansing Michigan area in 2011. Since 2012 she has served the Troth as the Michigan Steward (2012-14), the Wisconsin Steward (2014-16), and the Ohio Steward (2015-18). In 2017 she joined the Rede and completed the first year of the Troth's Lore Program. She was ordained as clergy by The Troth in 2019. A strong believer in Inclusive Heathenry, Snow works with several prisons, interfaith groups, and coalitions to promote the Troth's vision and mission.

In her secular life, she holds a Masters Degree in Human and Community Resource Development and serves as the Executive Director for a local nonprofit. She is married to a fellow Troth Clergy member who just happens to be her soul mate. Together, they have a dog, no kids, and a commitment to leave the world better than how they found it. Snow works primarily with Skadi, Freyja, and Odin, and finds that between the three of them, she has more than enough on her plate.

About the Cover Artist

Timothy "Bjorn" Jones, a traditional carver, currently lives on the East Coast of Canada. He draws on historical sources to portray characters from Norse and Anglo-Saxon folk tales, legends and ancient religion through his wooden sculptures. Timothy's aim is to use these figures as they were originally intended—as a way to communicate ideas and teachings.

www.ingramcontent.com/pod-product-compliance
Lightning Source LLC
Chambersburg PA
CBHW031419040426
42444CB00005B/637